Dinner
with
Jesus

*and Other Left-handed
Story-sermons*

Meeting God Through the Imagination

Dinner with Jesus

and Other Left-handed Story-sermons

DONALD F. CHATFIELD

Ministry Resources Library

Zondervan Publishing House • Grand Rapids, MI

Dinner With Jesus and Other Left-handed Story-sermons
Copyright © 1988 by Donald F. Chatfield

MINISTRY RESOURCES LIBRARY is an imprint of Zondervan Publishing House,
1415 Lake Drive, S.E., Grand Rapids, Michigan 49506.

Library of Congress Cataloging in Publication Data

Chatfield, Donald F.
    Dinner with Jesus and other left-handed story-sermons.

    Includes bibliographical references.
    Contents: Dinner with Jesus—The greatest gift—The sign of Jonah—[etc.]
    1. Story sermons. 2. Sermons, American. I. Title.
BV4307.S7C48   1988   252'.051   88-13672
ISBN 0-310-52021-5

Edited by Michael G. Smith
Designed by James E. Ruark

Printed in the United States of America

91   92   93 / CH / 10   9   8   7   6   5   4   3

For
AMY and GREG
who have always
preferred stories

Contents

Introduction

A left-handed sermon is one that encourages the right side of the brain to take the lead for a while. The right hemisphere of the brain governs the left side of the body; so what I call left-handed sermons tend to come from and speak to the right side of the brain more than the left. The brain's right side experiences life by way of story and sense experience:

> The right side of the brain is the wholistic hemisphere. . . . its process is . . . less defined, less precise, more global. . . . The left brain is a patterning of imperative and of directive proclamation. The right brain is a patterning of the presence. "Do this and you shall live," versus "Open your hearts, open your eyes, open your ears, and be in the presence of God."[1]

We need both sides, of course. But typical sermons tend to favor the logical, imperative side, rejecting the rich texture and flavor of a lot of the Bible itself—which is largely and basically *story*. One excessively right-handed old Puritan divine once complained that "much of Scripture is in the form of story, for what reason the Holy Ghost himself best knoweth." He voiced a distrust of half of the human mind, a distrust that still haunts our culture and our faith.

Sometimes in preaching class, students who have been

---

[1] James B. Ashbrook, quoted in an interview reported in "Worship on the Right Side of the Brain," by Tim Quinlan in *Aware*, Garrett-Evangelical Theological Seminary News and Information for Alumni/ae and Friends (Spring 1983): 6–7.

challenged to include picture, event, and story in their excessively logical, propositional sermons, look around helplessly in frustration. And even as they are doing so, there is the sound of the wind at the window screens, pushing its way in to play at lifting the edges of the pages of those sermon manuscripts lying on their desks. Fortunately for those student preachers and for all of us, a current emphasis on story in the doing of theology is urging us to recover our heritage:

> Humankind needs theological stories because human beings are fundamentally interpersonal and because, if the Christian God's promise is true, then humankind is fundamentally related to God as person. Since story is the only means by which the interpersonal reality of humankind can be expressed in its cognitive and affective fullness and since our relationship to God is fundamentally interpersonal, it follows that storytelling and storylistening provide the most appropriate means of enabling us to live this relationship.[2]

I have always loved stories, certainly from the time that my mother would read my Winnie-the-Pooh books to me over and over again—and probably from long before that. I love hearing them, making them up, telling them, reading them, watching them, being in them (I acted for many years, and have directed for more). I think in picture, plot, event, and place. I am right-handed, yes; but I carry left-handed genes. I can do abstract work, but never with the ease and comfort and confidence with which I enter the world of a "cracking good tale," the world of story and the wholeness of experience, the eventful peopled world of my right brain.

My schooling persuaded me (and many others) that the logical and abstract side of my mind had the most value; and I believed it, all the way through a fairly abstract graduate thesis. But when I was done with that, half of me was numb. The years since then have been a journey of finding my way back to the world I had left behind: the world of story. It is almost like

---

[2]John Navone and Thomas Cooper, *Tellers of the Word* (New York: Le Jacq Publishing, 1981), xvi–xvii.

the journey of those whom the schoolteachers tried to break of their left-handedness in the bad old days, after which they had to struggle back to valuing themselves as whole people. So for me, telling more and more sermons as stories has been part of coming back home to myself.

Several years ago when I became interim preacher to the Northminster Presbyterian Church in Evanston, Illinois, I decided that I would compose my sermons entirely orally. Working without notes pushed me to structure my sermons more like plots, and with more images and events, than I did when I used to write out sermons in advance. I began to use more plot and picture, whether the sermon was primarily a story or whether it wasn't, which was usually the case back then. It was just too hard to remember the old propositional kind of sermon when I didn't have any written guides to help me. A few times I told a story as the whole sermon, and I regularly made up stories to tell the children. As a farewell gift when my time there was up, the congregation presented me with a beautifully illustrated copy of the book *World Tales*.[3] That gift said to me, "You are a storyteller." I've tried to listen to what they were telling me.

I continued to tell tales as sermons occasionally, at the First Presbyterian Church of La Grange and the Palatine Presbyterian Church, both in Illinois, where I again filled pulpits during interim periods between ministers. Then several things came into my life: John Aurelio's book, the children in Elk Grove Village, and most of all, Reuven Gold. Reuven came first, but I didn't fully realize his importance to me until later, so I'll talk of him last.

John Aurelio wrote a fascinating book of story sermons called *Story Sunday*.[4] In it he told how the captive restlessness of

[3] Idries Shah, comp., *World Tales: The Extraordinary Coincidence of Stories Told in All Times, in All Places* (New York: Harcourt, 1979). I wish every storyteller had a copy of this marvelous book.

[4] John Aurelio, *Story Sunday: Christian Fairy Tales for Young and Old Alike* (Ramsey, N.J.: Paulist Press, 1978).

11

the children at the Masses he was celebrating moved him to have "story Sunday" once a month. On that day the children could come forward and sit around him, and in place of a regular homily he gave what he called a "Christian Fairy Tale." At the Elk Grove Village Presbyterian Church, where I was then preaching, the Christian Education Committee asked if the children could stay for the entire worship service. I thought it was a wonderful idea, and I immediately adapted Father Aurelio's plan. One Sunday a month was to be our story Sunday. The adults loved it (almost everyone seems to love stories), and every time I announced that this was a story Sunday, you could see all the grown-ups suddenly relax. When we caught that, we all laughed.

Several years ago, at a meeting of my professional association, the Academy of Homiletics (don't you love the name?), I first heard Reuven Gold, Master Storyteller. He was the evening's "entertainment."[5] I watched and listened as a man who had never met me told stories—mostly Hasidic tales—that moved me to my depths. I laughed and I cried, but most important, I could feel something, in my body as well as in my mind, opening up as he talked.

Since that time I have realized that he was able, by telling us *his* stories, to tell me a part of *my* story that I had never heard before.[6] One result is that I have increasingly found that I too am a teller of stories. And more than that: I am told by the stories I tell. And most of all, in the telling of tales I can increasingly see my life as a tale told by God.

So here we are. Again I am preaching at the Elk Grove

---

[5] A few years later, when I began to understand what his storytelling had really meant in my life, I invited him to the place where I teach to tell stories for an evening. He asked the people there why they had come. One person answered, "I just came to be entertained." He laughed his infectious, wheezy laugh. "Oi vey!" he said. "Are *you* in trouble!" He was right. To listen as a skilled and devoted storyteller involves us in a great and important tale is to risk some kind of transformation. Great tales and great telling are never just "entertainment."

[6] Reuven Gold is still telling stories and may be contacted at P.O. Box A3769, Chicago, IL 60690.

Village Presbyterian Church; and again I find on story Sunday that the tales I tell are telling out my life, bringing me new knowledge, and pointing me on down the road. For years I thought I *ought* to write a book about preaching (and didn't, of course). Then I thought of the tapes of my story sermons, and this book just began to happen, as I transcribed one sermon after the other and experienced again the delight of these stories that had, through me, grown into the world. The dean and the president, together with the Committee on Faculty of Garrett-Evangelical Theological Seminary in Evanston, where I teach preaching and worship, graciously granted me a sabbatical leave to finish the project.

But it's hard to finish with stories. More keep growing, crowding into the world through me. Maybe some day we can get together again . . . say, for *breakfast* with Jesus.

DONALD F. CHATFIELD
Redlands, California
August 11, 1988

Dinner With Jesus

This is the only piece in this collection that was written down beforehand and read to the congregation. I proceeded this way because it takes the form of a memo. As I began thinking about what it must have been like for Levi the son of Alphaeus to leave his job abruptly one day, it seemed as if a memo of explanation to the boss would emphasize the oddity and the power of it in a way that contemporary people, especially those who have to contend with memos a lot, would appreciate.

Scripture sometimes seems so inexorably *back there*. That means it often doesn't connect with our own lives, which we live *up here*—except when we're feeling "religious." But it cannot have been like that for the people who first met Jesus. Even though some of them left their regular jobs to follow him, he in no way removed them from their world or from their ordinary selves. They didn't leave their world to go find him; he entered their world and found them. That is how they and their world came to be transformed.

I believe Jesus works the same way now. But how can I reflect that in my preaching? How can I take stuff from back there and let it enter our lives up here? How can I let people *feel* it? How can *I* feel it? In this instance, I do it by putting Matthew's reflections in the modern form of a memo and by inserting details that come out of our contemporary life. After hearing this sermon, one man told me that I was now enrolled as a member of the Society for Creative Anachronism. I like that.

15

Dinner With Jesus

(Mark 2:13–17)

And as he passed on, he saw Levi the son of Alphaeus sitting at the tax office, and he said to him, "Follow me." And he rose and followed him (Mark 2:14).

MEMO

TO: Chief Collector, Capernaum Tollhouse, Interior Receiving Section

FROM: Levi ben Alphaeus, former collector

SUBJECT: Resignation

Dear Howie:

I know I should have gotten this memo to you two weeks ago, when I actually did this crazy thing, but there just hasn't been time. I know, I know, you probably figure what with me gallivanting around the countryside, eating and drinking and listening to the Boss teach, I should have had plenty of time to drop you a little note. Edgar saw me Monday and said you were really steamed that I didn't let you know whether I was coming back. Boy, that gave me a real guilt trip! To think you've been saving me a place all this time. . . .

But I did want to write you more than just a few lines: "I

quit. Your Friend, Levi." I mean, you might think I didn't *like* working in the Interior Receiving Section. But the IRS has been good to me, and you've been a great boss, and a real friend as well. So I figured you deserve more of an explanation.

Thing is, Howie, I couldn't figure out how to explain this whole thing so you could understand it. I mean, this guy comes barging into the office that Wednesday morning, walks right over to my station—where I'm arguing with Joseph ben Jacob about the valuation I'd just put on the four jars of spices Joseph was bringing in from Damascus—and the guy says to me, he says, "Follow me"!

Well, this I don't need, because Joseph is giving me a real hard time. (So what if I valued them a little high; Joe and I both knew what he was carrying in the false bottoms of those jars, and it certainly wasn't his dirty socks!) So I said, "Just hold your horses, Mac." That was when I noticed these four other guys with him, giving each other looks when I said that—looks like, "Who does he think he is *talking* to like that?" But you know how it is, Howie, when you sit at the custom desk, you're king, and folks just got to wait until you're good and ready.

Oh, I forgot to tell you about these four guys. They were fishermen. I knew *that* much as soon as they blew in the door! But the main guy, I couldn't figure; looked like a worker, though. (Turns out he'd been a carpenter over in Nazareth with his old man.) Anyway, these four guys were Simon and Andrew, and James and John. I recognized them. Now, this wasn't the Sabbath, it was a work day; so what were the owners of the two largest fisheries on the north coast doing, wandering around like four guys on welfare? Started me wondering: Who *was* this bozo, anyway?

(Howie, I'm afraid that kind of distracted me, and I quit listening so good, and when I came out of it I realized Joseph had really beat me down. You'll find the paperwork on my desk. But don't hassle him about it. Next time you see him, tell him Levi says, "God bless." That'll blow his sandals off!)

So Joseph goes off, and I turn back to this guy, and as I do,

I hear James ben Zebedee say something to him and end up calling him "Rabbi." Well, naturally, I get up; I would've in the first place, if I'd have known he was a teacher of God's Law. I mean, I may not have time to study it or keep much of it, but you gotta show a little respect! So there I am face to face with this guy, and he's just waiting patiently for me, and I get a really good look at him. People who've never seen him think he must really look different, but he doesn't. Just an ordinary-looking guy; the difference I guess is mostly in the way he talks. Like, when I suddenly remember that he said something to me a couple of minutes before, and I say, "What did you say?" And he just says it again: "Follow me."

Now this is the part I can't explain, Howie. I mean, is this crazy, or what? Guy wanders in and wants me to drop everything and go with him. I shoulda asked him a thousand questions, like, "Where are we going? How long? Can it wait until I can arrange a leave of absence? What's the salary? Fringes? (How's he gonna beat 30 thou a year plus all the bribes and skim-offs you can manage?) Do I get paid vacations? Who's gonna take care of my widowed mother?" (My ma just laughed when she read this part . . . I'm typing it at home . . . "Who's going to take care of *you* is more like it," she said.) But I didn't say *any* of that to him. I just pushed my chair back and followed him out into the street. Me, four fishermen, and a wandering rabbi! What the heck did I think I was doing?

Edgar calls out to me, "Hey, Levi? It's too early for your lunch break." I let it go. He owes me plenty of lunch breaks. Funny, isn't it, Howie? One part of me was thinking, I'll be back this afternoon. But my feet knew they'd never be parked under that desk again.

Well, as we walked along, it rose on up from my feet and dawned on the rest of me: This is a whole new life! This is really something big! Here I am, Levi the publican, the tax collector, not exactly the most popular man in town, and now I'm a rabbi's disciple. Wouldn't Simeon the Pharisee be surprised, I thought. He hates it that I even live in his neighborhood, me with my unreligious friends and our all-night parties. He hates all us people who don't keep Moses' law to the letter, figures it's because of us that Israel is under the lousy Romans; it's God's punishment 'cause I didn't tithe my pomegranates. And he hates us tax collectors worst of all, because we work for the Tetrarch, who cooperates with Rome. Wouldn't this give Simeon fits, I'm thinking, if he could see me hobnobbing with a real live rabbi. Here's one rabbi that sure doesn't pick his disciples for social class! Course, I think, as I look at Simon and Andrew, he doesn't pick 'em for bouquet, either. Whew!

Anyway, I guess it was thinking about old Simeon's eyes bugging out that makes me forget myself and go up to the Rabbi and say, "How's about dropping by my place for dinner tonight?" He just stops dead and looks at me, and I hear the four Mackerel Brothers stop behind me and suck wind through their teeth. And then I realize, Oh boy, have I put him on the spot! A real live rabbi asks me (me!) to be one of his bunch, and I embarrass him by asking him to eat with me. Not just come to my house, which would be tough enough, but to actually sit down at the same table and dip in the same dish with me, a publican. He probably eats kosher, prays every day, and goes to synagogue on the Sabbath. It's like asking him to eat with a Gentile, or worse, a Samaritan.

So I'm getting ready to say something like, "Of course, I know you're busy, got lots of teaching to do, busy schedule, no sense hiking out to the suburbs, why don't I just reserve a table at Rachel's Religious Restaurant and Seafood Emporium over there, save you a lot of . . . " But he just turns to the others and says, "Well, boys, what do you think of that?" And they kind of look at each other for a second, searching for something to say, and then big Simon (the Rabbi calls him "Petros"—the Rock), he bursts out, "Master, I think the shepherd who left the ninety-nine safe sheep has found one who was lost." And so the Rabbi throws back his head and roars with laughter, and all the others do too, and Rocky blushes bright red ("Tell you the story later," he mumbles to me). And the Rabbi throws his arm around my shoulders and says, "I'm going to call you 'Matthew' (Imagine! He calls *me*, a tax collector, the 'Gift of God'!). And Matthew," he says, "it will be a joy to come to your house for dinner tonight."

And that's when I remember, Howie—it's Wednesday! The weekly gathering of the poker club is at my house tonight. They'll be expecting a quiet evening away from the wife and kids, with pizza, beer, cigars, and dealer's choice; and what'll they get? A rabbi! It'll be a contest who'll walk out the door first, them, or the Rabbi when he gets a look at my collection of no-good friends.

I'm real itchy all afternoon, because I want to get back and see what magazines I have to hide. I even think of asking Simeon if I can borrow his house and servants for the evening, that's how crazy my head is getting! Suddenly the Rabbi looks at me, and he says, "Matthew Levi, a man once gave a banquet and invited many people; but when the food was ready, they all made excuses to his servant, who returned with no dinner guests. The man was angry, so he sent his servant to drag people to the feast from bus stops, doorways and alleys, greasy-spoon diners—and tollhouses." I musta looked blank, 'cause then he says "Matthew Levi, it's time to go to your house for dinner." I'm thinking about what he said all the way to my place. A bunch of down-and-outs got a nice meal because some fat cats didn't feel like showing up. Did the Boss call *me* because somebody else, a Pharisee, maybe, turned him down? I decided that would be okay. This was about the biggest thing that ever happened to me: if I found it because someone else dropped it, well, finders keepers losers weepers I always say.

As we came up the road, I saw Simeon studying the Law in the neat little courtyard in front of his house. When he saw us coming, he looked for a long time, and then it was like he recognized the Rabbi, because he suddenly jumped up and ran in the house. I guess he had a few phone calls to make. We trooped into my place, and that's when it all really came to a head. Fast Eddie was already there, practicing his one-handed triple cut. Sam had already popped a beer and was working his way through *Playboy*. (He wasn't always there; this week he had Wednesday night off from tending bar at the Capernaum House.) Jocko was making some entries in his little black notebook that we all knew not to ask him about. They all kind of looked up when we waltzed in the door, and Fast Eddie fanned the air away from his nose when he got acquainted with the aura of the Four Friendly Fisher Folk.

"Guys," I said—I had to say it twice before I got the word out from from where it was stuck in the back of my throat— "I'd like you to meet some new, uh, friends of mine, maybe you know these guys from the fish market? Simon ('Call me Rocky,' he said with a broad smile, as he stuck out one big paw) and his brother Andrew; and these here are James and John, the sons of Zebedee. And this," I said, taking a deep breath, "is . . . our, uh, rabbi, you know, our teacher, um, uh . . . "

"Jesus," he said. And then he went to each of them, got their names, started talking with them. Boy, the looks I got! In the middle of this I heard the air horn as Jimmy and his partner the Jericho Kid pushed their eighteen-wheeler up in front of the house. Well, I just couldn't take any more, Howie, so I ran into the kitchen and worked off some uglies by hollering at the servants for a while, got 'em rustling up extra food and stuff. When I came back in with the dip and chips, I stopped dead in the doorway. All the guys were sitting on the floor, and the Boss was sitting on the sofa in front of them, making like a rabbi. Only, he didn't talk a lot of religion like the scribes and teachers of the Pharisees usually do. Like, when I came in, he was telling them this story; I never will forget it.

"A Pharisee and a tax collector," he said (glancing at me), "went up to the temple to pray. The Pharisee went right up front, confident in his own virtue. The tax collector was on his knees, 'way back by a pillar. The Pharisee was glad in his heart, and prayed like this: 'Dear God, I thank you that I am a good man, keeping the law, keeping myself pure and holy for you, praying for your holy people and for Jerusalem, tithing to your temple from all that you have given me; thank you for giving me the light of your law to guide my steps, so that I am not unrighteous, or an adulterer, or a sabbath-breaker, or an idol-worshiping Gentile, groping in deep darkness; I thank you that I am not an extorter of money and oppressor of the poor of my people, like that tax collector back there, never lifting a finger to keep your holy law. Who does he think he is, even coming in here to your sacred temple?' "

Jesus looked up at me as he said these words, Howie, and it felt like he was looking right into the heart of my shame. Who *did* I think I was, pretending to be a rabbi's disciple? I had never paid the slightest attention to God! A couple of the guys were looking at me, and that's when I realized that there were tears on my face. I just let 'em be, stood there holding the dip and chips.

The Boss went on: "But the tax collector didn't even lift up his eyes to heaven, but beat on his chest, calling softly, 'God, have mercy on me, a sinner.' " Then Jesus' voice got a tone in it that made us all hold our breath: "Amen, amen," he said, "I tell you the truth: *this* man went home at rights with God, *and not the first!*"

See, Howie, that's when it happened. With a handful of words this guy opened a door to God for a bunch of rum-dums and fast operators like us. It was like he made us all his brothers. That's when I decided, I'm going with this guy wherever he goes. This is my Boss from now on. Maybe it seems crazy to some people; but when you've had heaven handed to you on a platter, and a new name, and a new family, and self-respect . . . well, you just gotta go with it.

Oh, I forgot to tell you, Howie, that just then I noticed Simeon the Pharisee and some of his cronies standing at the door, probably came over to holler about Jimmy and Jericho's rig standing out front. But I knew from the look on their faces that they had heard the last bit about the Pharisee who didn't get right with God. Boy, were they mad! But for some reason they stayed there, as if the Boss's teaching had a hold on them, too. So they listened to all he said (one of them was even taking notes), and they were there when the whole motley crew of us bellied up to the table. I saw Simeon turn green at the unrighteous assortment of food I'd scrounged up, but Jesus never blinked an eye. They watched as he sat down in front of that strange mess of food and folks, took the bread, lifted his eyes to heaven, and blessed God who had brought us the bread out of the ground. Then he broke it and passed it to each of us, and I tell you, that bread tasted better than any I'd had in years!

I can't describe the meal, Howie, too much happened. (It always does, when Jesus is around.) But once, when I got up to refill the glasses, Simeon waved me over to the door. You know, I felt so good, I said, "How's about you and your friends coming in and having a bite with us. I know the Rabbi will be glad to have you." But Simeon just looked at me and kept his toes firmly on the other side of my threshold, and I felt unclean and sinful next to all his purity, just the way I always did. But somehow I suddenly understood the look on his face. He was jealous! He wanted Jesus to be at *his* house. Here he was, the best man in the neighborhood (I gotta admit it; he really is!), and when a real live rabbi comes around, he comes to the house of a ripe old sinner like me!

So I saw the longing and the hurt in his eyes as he said, watching the Boss with his hand on Andrew's arm, "Why does your . . . your Master . . . eat with tax collectors and sinners? *We* are the God-fearing people. I don't understand!"

Jesus must have heard him from across the room, because he called out to him, "Simeon, people who are well don't need a doctor; sick people do." Then he said something that haunts me, I don't know why. "I didn't come to call virtuous people, but sinners." And he kept his eyes on Simeon's face, until Simeon turned on his heel and went back over to his place, him and his friends. You know, I think that made the Boss a little sad.

Well, that's about it, Howie. This guy has really turned me

around, and I'm with him from now on. I feel like I'd follow him to death, if I had to.

We're going off for a while, hit some of the other places around Galilee, pick up a few disciples, who knows? Just give Edgar my back pay, he can bring it by my ma. You know, I thought she'd throw a fit, me quitting and running off with some guru, but it turns out she and her bridge club had been driving over to Nazareth on the quiet to hear him for a couple of weeks, so she knew all about him before he shows up in Capernaum, thinks he's terrific, gives me her blessing and all. Rosie's really hot, though; says how are we going to get married now, me having no future anymore. She even cried. I felt like a heel, but I told her, you gotta hear him for yourself. She wasn't buying any. Well, someday, maybe.

So take care of yourself, Howie. Give my regards to the staff. I'll give you a ring when we get back to town. Have you out for dinner with Jesus.

The Greatest Gift

This is a Christmas gift for you. It's a story I made up. But fiction is not different from truth; fiction is only different from fact. This story is fiction, certainly; whether it is truth is up to you. If you ask me, How is this story related to the verse that is listed just before it?— the verse that quotes what Elizabeth says about Mary—I would be hard put to answer. I know that the beginnings of this story came to me as I was thinking about that verse. I guess perhaps the relationship lies in this, if anything: that Mary is given to us, at the Christmas season, as one of the blessings of God. Mary is given to us, who are so busy preparing for the coming of Christ, as a lesson.

We keep thinking, at Christmas especially, "Let us get ready for God." But what did Mary do to make ready? Did she even ask for this thing to be given to her? Could she even have dreamed of it? When you think of it, how could any of us have dreamed of the pathway of our own life, let alone of any of the other gifts of God that have been given to us in the course of it? No, this thing that happened to Mary came to her without any conscious action or preparation on her part, and it's perhaps the greatest gift that God can give.

The greatest gift of all is the gift of the presence of God, which comes to us this season, as at all seasons, in spite of ourselves and in spite of our activities, and not necessarily because of them. I guess the most we can say is, in all seasons we ought to keep alert. As the Lord who came so unexpectedly told us, "Watch, therefore. . . ."

And if you were to ask me, How in this story is God related to what is going on? I would probably answer, In the same way that God is related to every moment of our lives. That is to say, God is always present: in every conversation we have, in every telephone call, in every ornament (significant or insignificant) that hangs upon our Christmas tree, in every chance overheard remark, in every image the mirror throws back to us, in every loving action done by ourselves or by another. God is always present. And *sometimes* our eyes are cleared, our ears are opened, and we see, and we hear, that Presence.

The Greatest Gift
(Luke 1:39–55)

"Blessed is she who believed that there would be a fulfilment
of what was spoken to her from the Lord" (Luke 1:45).

They had eaten lunch and then had sat and talked for a long
time, the six of them. And almost as one woman they noticed
that the gray December afternoon was getting away from them,
the darkness increasing—a darkness emphasized among the
canyons of the city, a darkness visible and noticeable even here,
in the quiet interior of the restaurant. It was the restaurant
where it had been their custom to come for lunch at the
beginning of the Christmas vacation for quite a few years now.

Almost as one, they realized that obligations were pressing
them—home, family, preparations for dinner—and they began
fumbling their way through to an agreement about the check,
and gathering up their belongings, and getting themselves in
contact with their coats and their wraps.

As she was standing shrugging into her coat, Marietta
caught a glimpse of a familiar face in a mirror across the room
and realized that it was her own. She stopped a second before
she buttoned her coat to study the face (given to her now
almost as a stranger's): middle-aged; not unattractive; yet
somehow obviously single. She made a wry mouth at the

thought, and the mirror faithfully sent it back. She could see in the mirror a hint of her mother's eyes, smiling at her (in spite of the fact that her own face was not really a smiley one). She thought of her mother: her mother, who had lived with her for so many years.

And that reminded Marietta that now these last three years she had been alone. The third Christmas, alone. Alone without her mother's familiar presence; alone without the disagreements and the shared laughter; alone without the conversations and the silences—comfortable and uncomfortable; alone (and the smell came to her mind at the same time) without the Christmas cookies for which her mother had become so well-known, both at the school where Marietta and her luncheon companions taught, and in the apartment building where she lived. She could picture those cookies, even though she hadn't seen any of them for several years: stars and ornaments; gingerbread men with candy pearls for buttons; snow-frosted houses, and trees, and choirboys; carefully wrapped and taken 'round and given to special people.

She was alone. And that stark fact reminded Marietta that it had become her tradition every year after this luncheon to shop. Oh, not for others. That was long since taken care of, the presents wrapped and distributed to other teachers and to neighbors and sent off in the mail to two cousins and to one sister and husband and children in Oregon. No, not for others; today she shopped for herself.

The first Christmas season after her mother had died, she remembered, she had just sort of stumbled into it, coming out onto the darkening street from this same restaurant, watching her friends scurry for home, and finding herself suddenly alone in the world. She had wandered aimlessly through crowded stores, and in one, suddenly turning a corner, she had come upon a carved cuckoo clock. It was extravagant, but she bought it and took it home and set it under her tree, gaily wrapped, and on Christmas morning opened it: a present to herself. A present that reminded her of that one extra-special present her mother had always set beneath the tree, ever since Marietta was a child. The clock ticked now upon her wall, a constant companion . . . and the start of a Christmas tradition.

Last year she had deliberately set out to shop for herself after the luncheon. The jade ring she had found was still on her finger. This year, she wondered with a sense of expectancy, what would it be? The rest of the afternoon, and a quiet supper in a favorite restaurant, and perhaps an evening of looking lay ahead of her, to find just what gift she would give herself.

These lingering thoughts and the abstracted good-byes to her friends made her the last out of the restaurant. She was turning toward the stores when she noticed that one of the women still stood there, uncertainly, on the gray sidewalk.

"Marietta?" Louise said softly. "Have you got a minute?"

In spite of her readiness to go looking for her gift, Marietta was glad that one of her companions had not gone. "What is it, Louise?"

"There's something I . . . there's something I want to show you." Marietta fell in beside her as they began to walk.

"What is it?"

Perhaps emboldened by her friend's tacit acceptance, Louise only shook her head slightly. "You'll see."

They walked along, talking of this and that (they had been separated at the table), until they turned into the doorway of a building that Marietta did not immediately identify . . . when the opening door brought a puff of the interior air to her nostrils, and she realized, even before she saw anything, that she was entering a Roman Catholic church. *How did I know that?* she wondered, as her eyes confirmed what her nose had told her. *The smell of pews and service books is the same everywhere. Is it a whiff of the wax of all those votive candles? a memory of incense? a hint of the the smell of the sacramental wine?*

As she entered that unfamiliar territory—for she was an uncompromising Protestant herself, loyal in attendance and service at the United Church which was her spiritual home— she felt as stiff and awkward as she had felt (she suddenly remembered) at her first dance, where she had stood head and almost shoulders above the tallest boy in the place. Now it was her Protestantism she could feel, not in her mind but in her body, her body that felt so unfamiliar here; whereas Louise slipped into the church as one would into a pair of comfortable old slippers, her quickly ungloved hand going easily to the holy water stoup, her body adjusting automatically to the familiar little rituals of entering her church. Stiff, awkward, and puzzled, Marietta followed.

They turned aside, and came to a place where there was a bank of flickering votive candles, and a kneeler, and a statue clad in blue and gold. *Mary,* thought Marietta. *The Virgin Mary,* she corrected. *The* Blessed *Virgin Mary,* she smiled to herself, remembering Maureen, a Catholic friend from grade school (unthought of for so many years!), and how fiercely and reverently Maureen used to say those words. Then she saw the statue clearly, and she became so still she hardly noticed as Louise shyly touched her arm and smiled and then went forward to kneel. Hardly noticed that she was left standing, in her Protestant unbendingness, before the likeness of her who was also called "the Queen of Heaven."

But what was it that had struck her so? The face? It was calm, clear, gentle, utterly peaceful . . . but no, it was something else that had drawn her eye, caught her so unaware. Her eyes traveled down the statue, down the blue folds of the drapery, down the arm . . . and then it came to her: it was in the bend of the wrists of those outstretched, inviting hands. A totally feminine gesture. She had never seen a man bend his wrist in just that way. (*Perhaps the bones are different,* she thought vaguely.) Only a woman would extend her hand just that way, just so gracefully, just so invitingly, just so tenderly.

And it washed over her in a flood that brought the sting of tears to her eyes that in her own Protestant heaven there were only *men!* God: an old man with a long beard (well, she knew better, of course, but so she had envisioned him in her childhood, and so she saw him still, just now, when the thought first came to her mind). Jesus Christ: young, virile, strong, decisive, masculine—the Lord. She had loved him with a passion since she was a girl. But she realized now, for the first time clearly, a truth that had always been there: there was no one in heaven to whom she could talk, woman to woman.

And then the second thought came to her: *There was!* Her mother was there . . . her mother! And, half looking at the face of the statue, but knowing it was not the statue she addressed, she said, "Mama? I miss you." The tears welled, began to run down her face. "I miss . . . the cookies, Mama. I miss . . . being with you. I'm so lonely, Mama!" And as self-pity began to take its grip on her, something unexpected shook it loose.

She heard a voice; not with her ears, but at the back of her head. Almost she looked to see if the lips of the statue had moved. *What a headline that would make!* she thought, half-smiling through her tears. GOD GIVES SPECIAL VISION TO PROTESTANT SPINSTER IN CATHOLIC CHURCH. But the statue remained what it always had been, a symbol; a symbol that had evoked a dear and wondrous presence for her. The silent voice spoke clearly: "It's going to be all right, honey. It's going to be all right."

And at that, unexpectedly her tears began to dry. Just so, her mother had comforted her, from the time Marietta was a little girl until two days before her death. All at once she knew that her mother was not dead, but alive. And she knew more than that. She knew that underneath her mother's voice she had heard the voice of One far greater than her mother. One who was not just her Father in heaven, but her true Mother— and Friend and Companion and . . . One to whom she could talk, as well. Woman to . . . Woman. And the words came unbidden to her mind: "I believe in the Holy Ghost, the holy catholic church (*with small c's*, she smiled, —*and large ones, too!*), the communion of saints (*I love you, Mama!*), the forgiveness of sins, the resurrection of the body (*oh yes; of course, of course!*), and . . . and the life everlasting!"

"What?" said a voice . . . a regular one, this time. Louise stood before her.

Marietta managed to get out of the church, and at the doorway, after a moment, she said to her, "Louise? Why did you ask me to come along?"

Louise's face flushed and her eyes averted. "Never mind," said Marietta, "I think I know." Louise smiled and embraced her, all in a rush.

As they stood on the sidewalk ready to part, Louise said, "Aren't you going to go and buy that Christmas gift for yourself now?"

"Yes," said Marietta.

"What do you think it will be this year?"

"Cookie cutters."

The Sign of Jonah

Most of my story sermons are intended for adults. This one I preached mainly for the children in the congregation. I was influenced in my style a little bit by comedian Bill Cosby, and in my intention a lot by John Aurelio, whose book *Story Sunday* is a wonderful treat. Aurelio decided that once a month the homily at Mass would be a story that could be enjoyed by both children and adults. I liked the idea and decided to try it out in my own way for the story of Jonah.

I made Jonah a youngster mostly because I wanted the children in the congregation to have fun with it. They seemed to, judging by their expressions and reactions. But afterward I reflected that making Jonah a kid had three engaging side effects: it makes his prejudices even more obviously silly than the grown-up Jonah's are; it allows for a children's-story type of *fantasy* fish that no one has to try to make into the central point of the story and then spend time wondering how a fish could swallow a person; and the idea of the pocketknife made God's parting shot about the withered plant (in the original story) much easier for me—and so I suppose for others—to understand.

God (or the angel, or whoever he is) just kind of showed up that way in my mind; the size came first, and then the clothes. I was helped to keep him that way by the memory of the marvelous God-figure in G. K. Chesterton's intriguing novel *The Man Who Was Thursday* (Bristol, England: J. W. Arrowsmith, 1912), which first suggested to me that God might really not look as we expect.

35

Normally I don't explain things at the end of a story sermon. This time I did say a few words to the adults as follows. You might enjoy these words more if you wait and read them when you're finished with the story.

Jesus said that one of the signs of his presence was the sign of Jonah (Matt. 12:39; Luke 11:29). What is the sign of Jonah? Several things: Jonah was three days in the belly of the fish and came back, just as Jesus was three days in the earth and rose; when Jonah preached, people changed and started living better lives, just as they did when they heard Jesus preach; and Jonah himself began to learn how to love his enemies. (Maybe that last sign is the greatest sign of the presence of Christ that there is.)

Incidentally, I think Jonah and the man gave each other a hug, and that Jonah shared his last sandwich and his last grape drink with him. That's what *I* think.

The Sign of Jonah
(Jonah 3:1–5, 10; 4:1–11)

"That is why I made haste to flee to Tarshish; for I knew that thou art a gracious God and merciful, slow to anger, and abounding in steadfast love, and repentest of evil" (Jonah 4:2).

Once upon a time there was a boy named Jonah. Jonah lived in a town called Jerusalem. Now Jerusalem was one of the best towns around. You could ask anyone there, not just the chamber of commerce—anyone. "Yes sir," they would say to you, "this is one of the best towns around. Wonderful climate; good neighbors; people paint their houses at least every other year; they mow their lawns; everybody's very helpful—if you get a flat tire, no more than twenty cars will go by before somebody stops to help you. It's a very nice place to live, to raise your children, plenty of parks, good schools. . . . " And so it would go.

In fact, there was, as far as anyone knew, only one problem with this nice town in which they lived. And that was that about ten miles down the road was the town of Nineveh. Now Nineveh was a really bad-news place; just ask anybody in Jerusalem! They would tell you: "Aw, it's terrible down there! People get into fights, and they spray-paint on the walls, and they steal hubcaps, and I heard that somebody got murdered down there! They even come over here sometimes, and they set fires, and they do all kinds of damage. You just don't want to mess with them. It really is the only disadvantage we have here: the people down in Nineveh are really bad people."

Well, Jonah accepted all this—kids mostly believe what folks tell them about people they've never seen. But one day a couple of things happened to bring home to Jonah how bad the people of Nineveh really were. First of all, they kidnapped his sister. That wasn't what was so bad; it was that they brought her back! (He knew they had kidnapped her, because that was how she explained getting home so late that day.)

Jonah's sister was a real pest—in fact, Jonah often thought that she was a Ninevite in disguise. She made his life miserable! She took his stuff without asking; she ruined one of his best records one time; she and her girlfriends laughed at him on the way to school; she said he was funny looking; she said he had too much of an imagination . . . she just did all the awful things sisters usually do to brothers. Oh, she gave him a terrible time!

It was bad enough that the people from Nineveh sent his sister back; but the thing that really convinced Jonah how awful they were was the thing about his pocketknife. For many years Jonah had wanted a Swiss army knife. But first they said, "You're too young! You'll cut yourself!" And then after that they said, "Well, we can't afford to buy a fancy knife like that." So Jonah sent away a coupon from the back of a comic book. He sold two hundred cans of tennis balls and got to pick his premium, which was a genuine Swiss Army Knife. He loved it! It had all kinds of gadgets: it had little scissors, and it had a Phillips head screwdriver, and a leather punch, and four different blades, and a can opener, and everything. After Jonah got his knife, there was no more problem if something broke around the house; they just sent for Jonah and his Swiss army knife, and he fixed it.

Jonah put the knife on his bedside table every night when he went to sleep. One morning when he woke up . . . it was gone! Well, as you can imagine, there was trouble. Jonah cried for a long time, then he got mad and kicked things, then he sulked and pouted, and then, finally . . . he figured it out! He slept on the ground floor, and his table was right next to an open window. Somebody from Nineveh must have come to Jerusalem, reached in his window, and taken his knife. After that, he didn't dislike them anymore; he hated them!

One night about a week later, Jonah was getting ready to go to bed, and suddenly there was a large man standing in the middle of his room. (Jonah couldn't quite figure out how he got there.) He was an unusual-looking kind of person. He was one of those people who look like a big overstuffed chair; it just made you feel good to look at him. He had a face that looked as if it smiled most of the time; but it wasn't smiling now. He was dressed rather oddly: he had a pink shirt with green stripes on it, red suspenders, purple pants, and yellow shoes that curled up on the end and had a little bell hanging on each toe. Nevertheless, in spite of his funny clothes, somehow Jonah knew that this wasn't someone you laughed at; this was somebody who dressed and looked and acted any way he wanted to . . . and got away with it.

Jonah said to him very respectfully, "Good evening, Sir."

And the man said to Jonah, "Jonah, I want you to go down to Nineveh."

Jonah said, "What for?"

The man burst out, "I've been very upset with Nineveh!" (By this time, Jonah was figuring out that this was probably an angel; it didn't bother him that the angel was fat and dressed funny, because he didn't have any ideas about what an angel was supposed to look like.) "Yes," the angel went on, a little more calmly, "*very* upset. They are really some bad people down there. There's no question about it, it's not just a bad reputation; they are rotten from the ground up! So I've been thinking of various ways in which to destroy them."

"Oh boy!" said Jonah, clapping his hands. "What have you been thinking about?"

"Well, I've been thinking of raining fire and brimstone on them from the sky. That seemed like a good idea."

Jonah said, "Yeah, yeah! That'd be great!" (Thinking all the time of his knife that was gone—and his sister that wasn't.)

"And then I was thinking of having lightning strike each building, from the tallest to the lowest, burn 'em all down."

"That's really good," said Jonah. "You've got some wonderful ideas!"

"Then I thought—they're right on the seacoast, just the way you are here—I thought I'd have a monster come out of the sea and tromp on them for a while." (Jonah liked that one best of all. He put his hands between his knees and hugged them, he was so excited.) "But first," the man said, "what I want you to do is, I want you to go down there and warn them that I'm going to do this."

"Why?" Jonah demanded, his mouth hanging open.

"Why, to see if they shape up their act," said the man. And with that he went away, as if he had gone around a corner; except there weren't any corners in Jonah's room, and Jonah couldn't quite see where he went to.

Jonah muttered to himself, "Well, I'm not gonna do that!"

At that, the man came back around the invisible corner and said, "Take a look in the mirror, Jonah." Jonah looked in the mirror. His hair had turned green and was standing straight up on end. "That's just for openers," the man said.

Jonah said, "I think I'll go," and his hair went back down and turned to its normal color.

The next morning, bright and early, Jonah got out his backpack and put in five peanut butter and jelly sandwiches and three cans of grape soda, and he set out . . . but not to Nineveh! He wasn't going to warn a bunch of knife-stealers to save themselves! He went down to the waterfront and found the captain of the boat that took the mail out to the offshore islands. He knew the captain pretty well, because he often sat and talked with him. "Will you take me out to one of the islands?" he asked.

"Sure, Jonah," said the captain of the mail boat. "Always glad to have you along."

You see, in those days folks thought that land angels couldn't find you if you went out on the water. Seems silly, but that's what they thought. So Jonah thought he was going to get away from the man with the red suspenders and the curly yellow shoes with bells on the ends.

But no sooner had they gotten out on the water than the wind shifted around into the northeast, which anyone knows is trouble. Everybody put on their slickers and boots. Then the waves came and the winds blew and the sky got so dark you'd have thought it was night; it was just *terrible* out there! You had to hold on to a rope as you walked along the deck, or else you would have been washed clean overboard. It just got worse and worse, and everybody was really scared.

But right away, Jonah knew why it was happening. The angel was angry because Jonah wasn't going to Nineveh. He must have a larger territory than Jonah had thought, and he was throwing this big storm because he was mad at Jonah. So Jonah, who was an honest fellow and knew you had to tell the truth at all times even if the consequences were bad, went to the captain and said, "Excuse me. If you throw me over the side, the storm will stop."

The captain said, "I couldn't do such a thing!" But he was scratching his head as he said it and looking at Jonah kind of funny. The crew was all gathering around, and the captain asked Jonah, "How come this storm is happening on account of you and will stop if we throw you over the side?"

"Well," said Jonah, "God sent an angel to me yesterday— (when he said 'God' everybody said 'Ooooh!')—and he said for me to go down to Nineveh and tell 'em to shape up—(when he said 'Nineveh' everybody said 'Ssssss! Booooo!')—and I decided I didn't want to do it because they stole my pocketknife and I wanted the monster to come out of the sea and tromp on 'em—('Yay! Tromp on Nineveh!' shouted the crew)—"but"— Jonah went on, speaking very fast now—"if I told them and they shaped up, the monster wouldn't, so I ran away instead of doing what the angel told me to do, and I figure he sent this storm because he's mad at me, so if you throw me off the boat you won't be caught in the storm anymore 'cause it's just only meant for me." Jonah stopped, partly because he had run out of breath.

The captain said "Gee, it would really be a terrible shame to do something like that to a nice young fellow like yourself." But all the time he was saying this, he had hold of Jonah's ankles and somebody else had hold of Jonah's wrists, and the crew was counting out "A-*one* and a-*two* and a-*THREE!*" Jonah went over the side of the ship and down, but he never even hit the water. A big fish came up, went "glump!" and swallowed him. The big fish went right to the bottom and sat there with Jonah in his stomach.

Fortunately, it was a large stomach, and there was plenty of air (although it *smelled* something *awful!*). But it was very dark; and every once in a while, the stomach would rumble. This was a big fish, and it made a *big* rumble. Well, all this gave Jonah some time to think about things. He decided that although he was still mad at the people of Nineveh, he would probably rather go there and warn them, like the angel said for him to do, than sit in a fish's tummy for the rest of his life.

So he said quietly, "Okay, I'll do it." At that, the fish went up to the top, put its nose on the beach, and spit Jonah out on the shore. Jonah picked himself up, brushed himself off, and went on down to Nineveh. Sure enough, everybody was hitting on everybody else and spray-painting on the walls and setting fires and doing all that bad stuff.

Jonah said, as loud as he could, "You had better shape up, or else a monster is gonna come out of the sea and tromp on you!" (He still liked that warning the best.)

The people said, "How do you know that?"

Jonah said, "Because God told me."

Everybody went, "Ooooh!"

Then Jonah stomped out of town and sat on a hill. He took

his binoculars out of his backpack, ate a couple of sandwiches, drank a grape soda, and watched. He watched for a day and a half. And . . . everybody shaped up! They started loving each other; they took the spray paint off all the buildings; they rebuilt the things they'd burned down; they built a couple of churches; and they started to have prayer meetings and hymnsings. Jonah knew that the monster was not going to come out of the sea and tromp on the Ninevites; he was stuck with his sister; and he'd never see his Swiss army knife again.

Jonah went back home, slammed the door, stomped up to his room, and slammed that door too. Everybody knew better than to ask him things like where he'd been for three days, when he was so mad.

He sat down on the side of his bed. The man in the red suspenders appeared. Jonah turned away. The man said, "What's the matter, Jonah?"

"I *knew* it would happen! I *knew* they would shape up and you wouldn't let the monster tromp on them!"

The man said, "Look behind your nightstand."

Jonah glowered at the man and said, "Don't want to." The man looked hard at Jonah's hair. Jonah sighed. "Oh, all right," he muttered. He moved the nightstand . . . and there was his pocketknife! Jonah was so happy! He held it tightly in his hand and he started to cry. He said, "Oh, I thought I'd lost it forever!"

The angel said gently, "Are you happy to see your knife? to find it again?"

"Oh, yes!" Jonah sniffled.

"Jonah, all those people down in Nineveh, they were lost too. In fact, I thought I'd lost them forever. But now, Jonah— thanks to you—I've found them again, and they've found me, and that's something that makes *me* happy. Do you understand?"

"Yeah," said Jonah. "Yeah. I don't like it much, but I think I'm beginning to understand."

So It Was You All the Time

As I read the story of Abraham and Sarah, I noticed something odd. Abram left Ur of the Chaldees because his father was moving away from there, and *not* because he heard the voice of God saying, "Get your stuff together, Abram, because I am calling you from here today." Back in Ur, Abram didn't hear anything but his old man telling him it was time to be moving on. Abram doesn't *hear* the voice of God calling him until later on, in Haran. He never knowingly meets God back in Ur.

And yet, years later, when God shows up and tells Abram who it is that's been dealing with him all this time, God says, "I am the LORD who brought you"—not from Haran, but—"from Ur"! I thought about that, about a God who calls us and we go, only we don't know it is God and we don't hear a call; a God who guides our steps for years and years, and then a long time later shows up and lets us in on the secret. The story that resulted from mulling all this over I put together from bits and pieces of various people's lives; I doubt that many of them will recognize themselves.

After they met the grace of God, Sarai's name was changed to Sarah, and Abram's to Abraham, because no one escapes unscathed from an encounter with the One Who Is. Since Abraham is a good name (unreasonably neglected by us Gentiles), I have used it for my central character. The words of the title are from C. S. Lewis's *Screwtape Letters;* the lyrical passage that contains them is worth quoting at length. The senior demon (Screwtape) is writing to the junior tempter (Wormwood) about the things the latter's human

45

"patient" must have experienced just after he died and burst into heaven, escaping Wormwood's clutches:

> Perhaps you had hoped that the awe and strangeness of it would dash his joy. But that is the cursed thing; the gods are strange to mortal eyes, and yet they are not strange. He had no faintest conception till that very hour of how they would look, and even doubted their existence. But when he saw them he knew that he had always known them and realised what part each one of them had played at many an hour in his life when he had supposed himself alone, so that now he could say to them, one by one, not "Who *are* you?" but "So it was *you* all the time." All that they were and said at this meeting woke memories. The dim consciousness of friends about him which had haunted his solitudes from infancy was now at last explained; that central music in every pure experience which had always just evaded memory was now at last recovered.[1]

---

[1]C. S. Lewis, *The Screwtape Letters* (New York: Macmillan, 1953), 158–59.

So It Was You All the Time

(Genesis 11:31–32; 12:1–5; 15:1–2, 3–7)

And he said to him, "I am the LORD who brought you from
Ur of the Chaldeans, to give you this land to possess" (Gen.
15:7).

One summer afternoon when he was ten years old, Abraham
was playing baseball. There were two out, and one strike on
him already, when he caught a fast pitch on the sweet spot. He
knew deep down as soon as he made contact that they'd better
watch out in the next county. It just drifted up and away; it
looked for a while as if it'd never start coming down again. He
never hit a ball like that before, and he never ever hit a ball like
that again; but he never forgot that hit. What a hit it was! It was
so good, it almost didn't matter that it cleared the bases. It
almost didn't matter that because of it they won the game, and
that because of it, for nearly a week and a half, he was a
neighborhood hero. It was such a good hit that it almost didn't
matter that when his old man heard about it, he took the whole
family out for ice cream.

(When Abraham was fifteen, the youth minister at the
church came to visit and tried to get Abraham interested in
going to the youth group. But there were a lot of things that
Abraham was more interested in than the youth group; and

anyhow, he found the youth minister of the church to be excessively muscular and hearty. So he gave it a pass.)

When Abraham was twenty and in college, he went on a trip with the college glee club. They were in a distant city. They sang well: old numbers, new numbers, classical, folk. During the singing of a rather fine arrangement of the old sea chantey "In Amsterdam there liv'd a maid," Abraham looked out and noticed a young woman with really wonderful brown eyes looking at him from the third row. He also noticed that the rest of her looked as good as the eyes. After that song and the other songs and the encores, he and she managed to find each other somehow through the crowd. They talked for a while, and then they went out and had something to eat. They went on talking, and they stayed until the place closed. Then they went out walking through that city, and without realizing it, they walked all night (fortunately it was summer, or they might have frozen to death). They ended up leaning over the edge of a bridge, watching the sun come up. They exchanged names and addresses, but she and he never saw each other again. Part of the reason was that they wrote each other a couple of letters, and the letters weren't nearly as good as their conversation, and both of them had sense enough to realize that sometimes a song is so good that no encore could ever do it justice.

(When Abraham was twenty-five and in business school, he was accosted several times by an intense young fellow from Oklahoma, who had wavy blond hair and deep blue eyes, and who asked him if he had acknowledged and accepted Jesus Christ as his Lord and Savior. Abraham didn't understand what in the world he was talking about, so he didn't think any more about it.)

When Abraham was twenty-seven, he got married.

When he was thirty, and working his way up a corporate ladder, one rung at a time (sometimes it felt as if he were doing it in his bare feet), Abraham got a call from a friend of his from college who was working at a radio station in town. They went out and had lunch. His friend asked him if he'd like to go over and see the radio station, so Abraham stole a little time from the afternoon and went. As soon as he saw the inside of the radio station, he knew what he wanted to do with the rest of his life.

There was much that followed: many conversations, learning about the radio business, persuading his family and friends that he wasn't crazy, cutting the "demo" tape, taking the job rejections, finding a place that would accept his meager experience, moving his family from a city to a small town, where he started off as the night man on the control board of the local radio station.

But in the middle of it all there did come a moment when for the very first time he was alone at the "board," introducing a record, with the turntable turning and one finger on the edge of the record, ready to release it at just the right moment. Not everyone knows what it is to love letting a record start to spin at just exactly the right moment, but everyone knows what it is to love doing something. So we can understand what it was like to be Abraham at that moment . . . another moment he never forgot.

When Abraham was forty, he was sitting in the church that he occasionally attended. In the middle of a sermon in which he had a vast disinterest, the preacher said some words he could never afterward remember, and something clicked in his mind, and he knew that all of a sudden he had met Someone who had been looking for him for many years. He didn't make a big thing about it; he remembered hearing talk about "conversion" from that young fellow from Oklahoma he had met in business school, but instinctively he knew he wouldn't like talking about whatever this was that was happening to him. So, quietly, on his own, he tried to learn how to pray, and he read what he could understand in the Bible. He and his family joined the church, a fact that went almost unnoticed among their circle of friends . . . a circle that gradually began to change. He and his wife began to give of their time and substance to the church, and their interests began to shift little by little.

When Abraham was fifty, he got a job offer to be the host

of a local TV talk show in a different city. After talking about it with his family, he took the job. In all the time he had the job he never mentioned on camera that he was a Christian. But he chose carefully the topics and people who would appear on the show, and he tried always to be dealing with something that was good for people (especially the poor and oppressed of the world, in whom, he had found, the Bible seemed to have such a special interest). He did this successfully for a number of years.

When Abraham was sixty, he and his wife and another couple were out camping (of which he had grown very fond over the years), and they had all sat up talking late at night. While the rest of them were talking and the fire was dying, Abraham had stretched himself out at full length on the ground and was engaged in trying to count the stars. He realized that he was looking at more stars than he had ever seen before in his entire life. After a while, the conversation kind of ran down, the way conversations do around a campfire, and the others decided it was time to go to sleep. But when they called Abraham, he didn't get up. They shone a flashlight in his face ai.d saw that he was still looking at the sky, and around his eyes were puddles of tears. He didn't respond when they talked to him, though he would get up and walk where they wanted him to walk. But the tears didn't stop.

With reactions that ranged from alarm to terror, they bundled him into the van and got him to the nearest place where there was a hospital . . . a small one, in a small town. It took a while for the emergency room staff physician to get hold of a doctor they thought might be able to help Abraham, and when she came and examined him and found nothing physically wrong with him, she talked to his wife and friends for a while. The doctor was about their age, and it turned out that she was the lay leader in the local Methodist church. So after thinking about it for a while, she said, "I'm not going to give him anything. I'm going to make a phone call. Just let him lie in there for a little bit."

When the doctor came back, she said, "There's places to

put you all up. If it's okay with all of you, I'm going to take you all home; Abraham too." So they went to the lay leader's house, the tears still sliding down Abraham's face. They bedded him down on the sofa in the front room, turned out the lights, and then they all went into the kitchen to talk.

"What's the matter with him?" asked Abraham's wife. The Methodist lay leader ducked her head as if she were a little embarrassed.

"Well . . . I've only seen it once or twice before over the years," she said. "One of my friends runs a Catholic retreat house a few miles out in the country, and I've talked to her some about it. I think your husband is having a"—and here she mumbled, so they had to ask her to repeat herself. She finally got it out—"I think he's having a spiritual crisis." They all looked at her as if something had worked its way loose.

"A 'spiritual crisis'?" one of them ventured.

"It'll come out okay," she said. "Just let him be." So after they had talked for a little while longer, they all bedded down here and there.

When they got up the next morning, they found that the doctor and her husband were making breakfast and that Abraham, his eyes dry and clear, was eating with a remarkable appetite. They noticed little change in his behavior afterward, though he seemed even fonder of children than he had been, and more given to taking walks by himself. Aside from that, he was the Abraham everyone had always known.

When Abraham was seventy, at the urging of several of his friends he sought a publisher for a children's story that he had made up and had told, over and over, to his insistent grandchildren (and more recently, to two enchanted great-grandchildren). It was accepted and published, very well illustrated. It enjoyed a small success, and the children who read it were drawn into a kind of magic of words that helped them to know a little bit more about the world and what it all meant, and to love it a little more.

When Abraham was eighty, he got out of bed quite

suddenly one night, because he thought Someone had called his name, and so he left his body behind. He went a little way, not quite sure of his direction, and he met the Someone. (It was the same Someone the Hebrew people use to call "Yahweh," which means something like "the One Who Is.") Abraham went straight up to the Someone without fear. "I'm glad to meet you like this at last," he said happily.

"Same here," said the One Who Is.

"I want to thank you for calling to me in that sermon, when I was forty. And . . . and for meeting me in all those stars, and . . . for helping me with my work, and . . . and . . . I just wish I had known you earlier in my life."

The One Who Is just grinned. "Abraham," he said, "do you remember when you hit that ball for a home run when you were ten?"

"Yes," he said.

"Do you recall watching a sunrise with a brown-eyed young woman?"

"Yes!"

"Do you remember falling in love with the radio business?"

"Yes!!"

The One Who Is just smiled.

"Oh!" said Abraham, as the light dawned, "So it was *you* all the time."

"Yes," said the One Who Is.

The Pilgrim's River

I believe some form of story, and the more dreamlike and "mythic" the better, well suits that evocative, moving, portentous document we call the book of Revelation. We do the book a disservice, I think, by preaching about it exclusively in straightforward, propositional terms. That's not the way the book itself operates, nor how it gets its grip on us. Most of the explanations of the Apocalypse of John that I've read or heard are either silly or boring when compared with the thunder and glory of the original.

Admittedly, this story operates in a different way than Revelation does. Stories at their best aren't built according to some plan or model. They arise; they coalesce around certain central images. In this case, the image of that wonderful river in chapter 22 (an image that has haunted me for years) suggests, as its opposite, the drought that exists in desert places before the distant rains send rivers to bring the wilderness to blossom. The image of the river also reminds me of John 19:34: "But one of the soldiers pierced his side with a spear, and at once there came out blood and water." And so it goes, one picture pulling up another until I begin to see amid them all a possible plot. (In some of this I owe a lot to reading the works of Ursula K. Le Guin, particularly her novel *The Beginning Place* [New York: Harper & Row, 1980].)

In the Hebrew blessing that occurs in my story, the letters "ch" are pronounced at the back of the throat, like an aspirated "k"; roughly speaking, it goes "ba-*rooch* ah-*taw* ah-doe-*noi* eh-low-*hay*-noo, *meh*-lech hah-oh-*lahm,* hah-*mah*-tzee *leh*-chem meen hah-aw-retz." It is the traditional Jewish grace over the bread, which begins any meal, however plain; it is of great antiquity and is presumed to predate the time of Christ and to have been used by him. It means "Blessed are you, O Lord our God, ruler of the universe, who brings forth bread from the earth."

The Sunday I preached this, the choir sang the lovely anthem "As Torrents in Summer" just before the Scripture reading. The anthem is Sir Edward Elgar's setting of a portion of a poem by Longfellow. I hadn't known they would sing it, nor had I heard the piece before; but it flowed so beautifully with the story that I give it here:

> As torrents in summer,
> Half dried in their channels,
> Suddenly rise, though the
> Sky is still cloudless,
> For rain has been falling
> Far off at their fountains;
>
> So hearts that are fainting
> Grow full to o'erflowing,
> And they that behold it
> Marvel, and know not
> That God at their fountains
> Far off has been raining![1]

---

[1] Henry Wadsworth Longfellow, "The Musician's Tale," sect. 22, "The Nun of Nidaros," from *Tales of a Wayside Inn*.

The Pilgrim's River

(Revelation 22:1–7, 13–14, 16–17, 20)

> And let [the one] who is thirsty come, let [the one] who
> desires take the water of life without price (Rev. 22:17).

A time ago, in a land I have never visited except in dreams,
there lived an old woman in a little shack on the side of a
mountain. She had lived on the mountain all her life, had lived
in that same shack ever since she had married, and had stayed
there the many and long years of her widowhood. For all those
years she had lived in her little house with its packed-earth
floor and its log walls, all as neat as a bright sewing needle.
Outside she had a little patch of earth for herbs, which she used
sometimes to make poultices when a neighbor's child would
come to her with flesh that was swollen and stung from
pressing unwisely through nettles, or sometimes to make
potions for those with a heart that beat too fast, being sick with
love or with dread. There was another patch where she grew
her vegetables, and some rough ground where her little goat
foraged.

    The old woman had little, but she lived well enough,
trading apples from her tree, and some of the cheese she made
so expertly from the goat's milk, and charging any who could
pay for her simples—when the potions had helped to heal. All

in all, while her life was not rich, it was not poor; and while it was not happy, it was not sad; and while she had little, she possessed the mountain and the trees, and the air and the sun, and the green and growing things; and while her neighbors did not come around often, except when they needed healing, they did come around then. They needed her knowledge, but they were a little afraid of it, too, so mostly they avoided her. As she had grown older, she had become more and more accustomed to grumbling, so that she could listen to her own voice, since she so seldom heard others'.

One summer a drought came upon the mountain. For day upon day and then week upon week the heavens were shut up, and they poured down upon the earth beneath, and upon the unprotected heads of those who worked the earth, only the fire of the sun. The sky held no cloud, nor mist, nor even haze, but only brassy brightness, reflected and amplified sometimes by dust blown up by the wind. There was no end to it in sight. The crops withered; the herbs in the old woman's garden shriveled; the vegetables did not grow well, and she began to fear for her apple tree; and at times, because there was little forage and so little to drink, her goat blatted piteously. But she herself, who had seen all things and suffered many, went on without grumbling any more than usual.

She did notice that every day, when she went the few hundred yards down the hill to the common well, the rope had to be played out further and further before the bucket would splash into the water. One day, when she went down the hill, she found that many of her neighbors on the mountain were waiting around the well in silence. Grumbling as always, she pushed her way through them, took hold of the rope, and let it slide through her hands as the bucket dropped down into the well. Furthest of all it went today, and instead of splashing and bobbing into the water, it thumped. When she pulled it up, there was little water in it, and that brackish, and she had to drop and pull repeatedly to fill her own bucket even half full. When she had got as much as she could, she picked up her bucket and turned around to find that her neighbors now stood in a half-circle, blocking her from the path back to her cabin.

"Let me through," she said. But they didn't move. "Let me through!" she demanded, lifting the bucket out from her side, as if she might use it for a weapon to batter her way through.

The oldest man among them stepped forward and said to her, "We need your help."

"You need nothing from me," she snapped, and added, "I get nothing from you; why should I give you anything?"

"We need your help," he repeated doggedly.

"I've got nothing to give you," she said.

"We need . . . rain."

"Huh!" she snorted. "If you need rain, don't talk to me; talk to the sky."

"You know the old ways," he persisted. "Some of us can remember the things that you used to do."

"Never did anything," she said.

"We remember. Some of us remember that when we were in trouble in the old days, sometimes you would go up to the top of the mountain, where it is forbidden to go; and everything would be right after that."

"Never did no such thing!" she said. "Old tales."

"*I* remember," he said. "Some of us still do. And we need your help now; for the heaven is shut up."

She looked for a long time at the ground and then looked directly into his eyes. "I don't do them things no more," she said.

"We need your help."

"I found out something," she said.

"We need rain!" he said.

"I found out it's dangerous!" she said. "I don't do it no more. Threw all my stuff away! All I do now is a little healing."

"We need your help," he insisted, his voice breaking.

A young woman, whose face looked old, spoke from one side. "There's not enough to eat," she said. "I'm drying up, and my baby is going to die." At that, something tugged at the old woman's insides; for one who has healed never finds it easy to restrain her hand when another is in need.

"We need rain," the old man insisted.

She looked again at the ground. Finally she muttered so that only those nearest to her could hear her. "I'll go back up to my cabin."

Then all the people moved aside and let her through, and the old woman trudged back up the hill with her half-bucket of water. When she reached her cabin, she closed the door, though it was hotter inside than out, and began to make her preparations. She set the water down by the fireplace. She went into the tiny sleeping room in the back; pulling and tugging, she moved an old bureau away from the wall. Hidden behind it was an opening dug through the wall and into the hillside. From the hole she took a kind of box, opened it up, and took out some things. Some of them you couldn't understand; some of them were jars and packets. Some smelled like dried herbs; a few smelled foul. The last two things she removed were a long-handled rattle and another handle with a whisk on it that looked like a horse's tail.

All these she carried out to her table. Then she pulled and tugged the table over by the fireplace and set everything in order on it. She built a little fire; she put the big black pot on the hook, swung it over the fire, and poured the water from her bucket into the pot. The smoke from the fire began to rise up the stone chimney, the chimney that her man had built with his own hands so long ago when they were both young.

Little by little the old woman began to add things to the water as it started to simmer: a pinch of this, and a bit of that sprinkled across the top; a piece or two of dried smoked meat that she'd been saving for herself; and a little bottle of something that had a cork in it so tight she had to pull it with her teeth. Sometimes when she added something to the pot she would hum to herself on a rising note, and sometimes she would mutter something that sounded like words in an old forgotten language. Sometimes before she put something in she would hold it in her hand over her head and turn widder-shins—to her left—twice around before she put it in. When everything had gone in, she took the ladle down and began to stir. She stirred it, and she spoke to it, and she sang to it, through half of the day, until all was blended and ready.

Then she built up the fire, so that it leapt around the pot, and the smoke went up, and the mixture began to bubble, and the steam of it and the odor of it and the smoke from the fire rose up the chimney. Had you been outside you would have seen it rise in the still, hot air, up through the branches of the trees, whose leaves were already curled and brown, and up into the still air, where it curled around and began to hang almost like . . . oh, if you used your imagination you could see it almost like a rain cloud; but strange-looking, strange enough to make a person slink back to the edge of the forest and watch from cover, waiting to see what sort of rain could ever fall from such a cloud.

As the smoke rose and the odor and the steam, the old woman picked up the rattle and the switch. She held them up over her head and then out at the ends of her arms, and she began to dance in a circle around the room—only so old she was now, that it was more like a shuffle than a dance. Sometimes she would cross her arms, and sometimes weave the switch in a pattern, and sometimes shake the rattle. At every quarter of the room, at the compass points, she would say something in an old tongue. Two times around she went, and three, always widdershins around the room, to the left, against the nature and turning of the universe.

She had nearly finished the third circle and had four more to go, when there was a knock against the door. "Go away!" she said. "I'm doing what you asked!"

But a voice she'd never heard before—a man's voice, strong and full of power—came through the door. "Old woman, let me in! You know that what you are doing is dangerous."

"Go away!" she said. "You've no right here." She continued to dance, trying not to miss a beat or skip a turn.

"You will hurt yourself," the voice said.

"I'll worry about that!" she snapped.

"You may hurt others, and even the life of the mountain," he said.

"Well, this drought ain't exactly doing it no good," she snapped back, and she finished another turn.

Again came the knocking, louder than before. "Old woman, I am hungry. I would come in and eat supper with you."

"Ain't got nothing to eat!" she called out.

"You've got what's boiling in the pot." She almost stopped in her tracks.

"That's not for eatin'!" she whispered. "Never for eatin'! Not that!"

"I am hungry," he said. "The use you make of it is evil; but it would be good and lawful, given to a hungry traveler."

"Go away!" she said. "Got nothin' for you! Only got somethin' for the people who live hereabouts." She continued to circle, now almost through the fourth turn, and three more to go.

The knocking continued, like the fall of a great hand, shaking the side of her house. But now the voice was hoarse and weak: "Old woman, I need your help. I have a wound."

She stopped where she was. Twice now the healer had been called up in her, and again she could not refuse. Anyhow, if she did it just right, she could stop here, before starting the fifth turn, without breaking the circle. She held the switch and the rattle over her head, slowly lowered them crossed to the ground, and put them where her feet were. She stepped out of the invisible circle and walked around the outside of it to get to the door. She opened it.

What a figure he was!—his beard straggled, his hair matted, hanging on by both hands to the door frame. Where had he summoned up enough strength even to knock, let alone make that fearful noise on the side of her house? And wounded—ah, yes, he was. "Come in," she muttered grudgingly. "Maybe I can do something about that wound."

He stumbled across the threshold, almost falling, and caught himself by taking three more steps. And so, before the old woman could stop him, he had broken through the circle she had been weaving around the floor in the still, hot air of that little cabin, and had sunk to his knees in the middle of the floor.

"Ye've ruined it!" she all but shrieked. "Ye've ruined my circle!"

"It would have done you no good," the man said, gasping, as he hunkered there. And then, weakly, "I'm hungry. Bring me something to eat."

"I told you—I got nothing."

"Give me what's in the pot."

"You don't eat that."

"It'll not do you any other good now."

Grumbling louder than usual, the old woman went over, swung the pot off the fire, looked at the contents, and then, sighing, took the ladle and put some in a wooden bowl. Almost as if it were an afterthought she picked up what was left of the loaf of bread that she'd baked from the last of her flour the day before. She brought both to him and set them on the earthen floor in front of where he sat.

"And yourself," he said, in a voice so low she could hardly hear him.

"What?"

"A bowl for yourself. I would not eat alone."

She went back over by the fire and ladled out the rest of it. With that any hope for spells was gone, for she doubted there would be any more water in the well to brew the potion that must steam into a cloud as she did her dance of summoning. Resigned, she carried her own bowl over to where he was, and she hunkered down in front of him.

When she was settled, he reached out both his hands and

61

picked up the loaf of bread. He held it in front of him, and he looked up, and he said, *"Baruch atah adonoi elohenu, melech ha-olam, ha-motzee lechem min-ha-aretz."*

"An old tongue," she said, her voice low. "I've never heard it. Do you do spells yourself?"

"I know no spells," he answered, as he broke the bread and handed her half of it. "But I do know how to say thank you to the One 'who brings bread out of the ground.' Most of the time I say it in my own tongue, as I learned it at my father's table when I was a lad." He paused a moment. "He was a carpenter," he added quietly. And with that he fell to and ate bread and broth, and at length he mopped the bowl clean. Then he rocked back a little, his hand to his head, as if he were dizzy.

She put down what was left of her portion, and she rose. "I'll get something now for that wound," she said. But by the time she had got back to him, he had fallen his full length on the ground, the wound underneath him, pressing against the earth of the floor. As thin and wasted as he was, he was still too heavy for her old arms to turn. So she sat down on her stool by the fire as the shadows lengthened out into the evening, and she waited till he should wake again and she could tend to his wound. But it was dark outside and warm by the fire, and her belly was full for the first time in a while; and she slept. And somehow, by the time she got her eyes open, it was morning, and the man was gone.

But the old woman smelled something familiar—the smell that is no smell. She got up and went over to where he had been lying, and there, just where that terrible wound had been pressed against the ground, she saw water coming up: a fountain from out of the flint heart of the mountain itself. A spring. Timidly at first, and then all of a rush, she put her hands down into the water; and it numbed them to the wrists, it was so cold. She cupped her hands and lifted it up and drank, there where she knelt. And it was the best taste of all, the taste that is no taste, which you can never remember and never forget. It must have been bubbling up for some time, because it had carved itself a little channel, and it ran out her door and on down the mountain.

She lived there, with that fountain in her house, some few weeks after that. And then, one day, she was gone. Some of her neighbors said that she had grown tired of living in a house that was so damp that mushrooms were starting to grow on the earthen floor. And some said she had gotten weary of people coming around and trampling her front yard into mud to get the water that flowed out from under her door, when they could have gone lower down and gotten it where the stream was broader.

But nobody was quite sure where the old woman went. Some said she had gone up to the top of the mountain, to the forbidden place, and there someone, or something, had taken her in exchange for the spring of water. Some thought that after working her spells, she must have gone off some place to die. One little girl claimed she had seen the old woman early one morning, carrying some things tied up in a bandanna. The girl said she had seen her setting off down the mountain, following the stream that becomes a brook and the brook that, they say, at the foot of the mountain becomes a river.

A man who sometimes had business in the village at the foot of the mountain came back one day to say that they told there of an old woman who had passed through sometime back. She would not stop, they said, for she was bound to follow that river wherever it might lead.

What If ... ?

I used to read a lot of science fiction, and I still have a fondness for the kind called "alternate universe" stories. This kind of story presumes that some crucial event in our past happened differently, and then shows us what the world is like today in that supposed alternative universe. Among my favorites in the genre is *Bring the Jubilee,*[1] which shows us present-day America in a world where the South won the Civil War. And my all-time favorites are the Lord Darcy stories by Randall Garrett (too few, alas!), one of the first of which was *Too Many Magicians,*[2] which takes place in a world where humanity has learned to approach the world with a scientifically controlled exercise of magic rather than with physical science. In Garrett's stories, late-twentieth-century Europe is still united under one crown and church, rubber-tired hacks are pulled by horses through gas-lit streets, and Lord Darcy is a criminal investigator who solves crimes with the aid of Master Sean O Lochlainn, a forensic sorcerer.

Well, here I was, looking at this story of Jesus rebuking Peter for trying to persuade him not to go and get himself killed, and I suddenly came all over funny. What if? We now know how the Christ story turned out, so to us it seems foreordained and set in stone; it couldn't possibly have happened any other way. But Jesus was obviously just as free as we are (else he was not human, and so

---

[1] Ward Moore, *Bring the Jubilee* (New York: Ballantine, 1953).
[2] Randall Garrett, *Too Many Magicians* (New York: Ace Books, 1983).

no use to us as a Savior). We think, "He *couldn't* have said "yes" to Peter and "no" to the cross."

He *could* not? We know that he *did* not. But if he *could* not, he was a puppet! I am convinced that when the Tempter set the easy way before our Lord, Jesus was *really* tempted; and when he groaned aloud in Gethsemane, he was *really* frightened; and when they came for him with spear and torch, he longed to "pass through the midst" of the temple guard and go on living, just as he (quite properly) had walked away from the murderous crowd that day on the hill above his hate-filled home town.

So I believe Jesus had a *real* choice when Peter urged him not to die, and no script in his hand or prompter in his ear, telling him in advance the gospel story we take so for granted today. *While he was living it, Jesus' life was one of real, and not seeming, decisions.* To make the wonder of that more clear, one day I asked myself this apparently simple question: What if the cup *had* passed him by; not later, in Gethsemane, but that day on retreat with the Twelve, up north in Caesarea Philippi?

What if . . . ?

What If ...?
(Matthew 16:13–28)

"God forbid, Lord! This shall never happen to you" (Matt. 16:23).

I'm Simon Peter. Some of you will remember me. I was Jesus' right-hand man for many, many years. You've probably heard the story about how Jesus picked his followers, and you certainly know all the glorious things he did through the thirty years that he was head of our nation of Israel. But not all of you know that his illustrious career is really largely owing to me. That's right! If it hadn't been for my reasoning with him that day at Caesarea Philippi, none of this would have happened.

That day he took us, his disciples, on a kind of a retreat far to the north. Later, in an isolated spot, he sat down with us and started talking about what the people thought about him. And then he asked us what *we* thought about him. Well, I told him straight out, "Jesus, I think you're the Messiah, the Christ, the one that everyone's been waiting for, the one who's going to change things and make things better; the one who's going to really turn this nation around."

Jesus listened carefully to what I said, he praised me for it, and then—I know you'll find this hard to believe—then he told us that his idea of being the Messiah was that he was going to go down to Jerusalem and suffer many things from the elders and chief priests and scribes, and even be *crucified!* Then he added some nonsense about rising from the dead on the third day, but everyone knows that's impossible.

I took him aside, away from the others, because I didn't want to embarrass him by having them hear this, and I really scolded him. I said, "God forbid Lord! This shall never happen to you."

He lashed out at me. He said, "Get behind me, Satan! You are not on the side of God, but of people."

I said, "You can call me names all you want to, Lord, but you're just not thinking clearly. There's something morbid about this idea. Why is it that you want to die?"

"Peter," he said, "I've studied the Scriptures and I believe that I am the Messiah, and that it's God's will for me to die for all people."

I said, "Now think about it for a minute, Jesus! You've got a following of thousands and thousands of people. Every place you go the whole area is jammed with the folks who come to see you. You've got a bigger following than anyone I've ever heard of. With that kind of constituency, Lord, you could do a tremendous amount of good. But not if you die! What use will you be to anyone then?"

He said, "I mustn't think of my own selfish advantage and my desire to live."

"But Lord," I protested, "it isn't selfish to desire to do what's best for helping people. You're not going to help anybody by dying. The people who've followed you and started to put their hope and trust in you, they will just feel betrayed. They'll drift away, and all the good you've managed to do so far will be forgotten. And what of us, your disciples? Like the rest of them, I left everything to follow you because I believe you are the one we've been waiting for, the one who's going to make a transforming difference in this world.

"Besides that, I have to admit it: I love you. We all do, all your disciples, all the women who follow you, everyone. We'll be heartbroken if you should die—die for nothing—and leave us to pick up the pieces and bear the burden."

"I believe that it's God's will," he said.

"Lord," I answered, getting angry at his stubborn thoughtlessness, "your thinking is really messed up. Here you're planning to go down to Jerusalem and make some grandstand play and die on a cross, so everyone can call you a martyr, and leave the rest of us alone and leaderless. Your cause would be hopelessly wrecked!"

We talked about it for quite a while, until I could see that he was beginning to listen to me. So we went back and talked with the others about it, and they were as shocked as I had been. Finally I suggested that we put it to a vote. So we did, and everyone was unanimously against Jesus going down to Jerusalem and dying on a cross.

"Well," he said (and I suspect he felt kind of relieved), "all right. I'll submit myself to the majority; that certainly is a way to find out God's will. So what do you suggest?"

We talked most of that day, and finally we came up with the plan that now everyone knows about. We worked for a few more months building up an immense following in Galilee, and then we went down to Jerusalem for the Passover, with thousands and thousands of followers. We made a triumphant entrance into the city with Jesus riding on a powerful warhorse and everybody shouting, "Hosanna," the ancient greeting to a king. The authorities were really impressed, and they watched carefully while Jesus sat in the temple teaching and gathering new throngs of people from among the residents of Jerusalem as well as from those who had come from other areas, and even from among the Jewish pilgrims who had come from all over the world.

While he was doing that, we disciples split up. Some of us went to the Sadducees, the temple authorities; some of us went to the Sanhedrin; some went to the leaders of the Pharisees; and some went to the most important scribes. We tried to achieve a working coalition. We convinced them that the people would follow Jesus and listen to him; that Jesus' message would be one of reconciliation and peace, and that he could bring together our whole nation. That way we would be able to have some influence with the Romans and improve conditions for everybody.

Well, it took two or three days, but we got the coalition put together. The throng that was gathering around Jesus became bigger and bigger. We went to see the Roman governor, Pontius Pilate (some of you might remember him). He'd become quite nervous about such a large crowd surrounding one man, and he was thinking about taking some sort of police action, but we convinced him that Jesus was a reasonable person who would listen to the viewpoints of others (just as he'd listened to mine!).

I put it to him straight. I said, "Pilate, you know it's almost impossible to govern this region. You know the trouble that you've had—the rebellions, the passive resistance, the demonstrations, the generalized hatred of Roman authority—but Jesus is one who teaches peace; and when he teaches, the people listen! He can bring everyone together, and if you're willing to make a few concessions, this whole area will be at peace. And *you* will get the credit from Rome." Well, he was impressed, and after a good deal of cautious discussion and haggling, he went for it.

We got a lot done during those years. The roads were improved; taxes were reduced; there was better care for children; medical care improved; new synagogues were built; education prospered. So many of the things that make life better for people became realities, and all because of the influence of Jesus. After this had been going on for a while, people were so impressed with Jesus' leadership that we worked up a new plan.

As you know, we Jews hadn't had a king for generations and generations, and Rome had always denied us the right to have one from the time they took us over. But we thought they might accept Jesus as king, since he was obviously no threat to their empire, and that way we could get even more accomplished. Well, Rome was interested, but unfortunately they still wouldn't buy the idea of a king—they were afraid some successor would arise and cause trouble in the future. But we got the next best thing. Jesus was named Prince! It was only for his lifetime of course, but it was magnificent! He moved into a palace with lots of servants. Some of us moved in with him, not for our own advantage, of course, but to be close to him so we could do even more good for the people.

Well, I don't have to recall the history of those wonderful years for you. I'll just say that sometimes I like to think back with pride and remember that in a sense really, I was the one who made it all possible. Without me Jesus would have died a martyr's death and been forgotten in six months. I sit here now sometimes by his tomb—a magnificent tomb it is—and look at the great stone rolled against the door. (It's sad to think that that stone will never move—never move again.)

I look at the inscription on the front of the tomb: Jesus of Nazareth, Prince of the Jews; and I remember. I remember the day when they brought word that he was dying. He was in his sixties. Bad heart, I guess. I went to see him, and he looked up at me and grasped my hand.

"Peter," he said softly, "I've been wondering."

"Just rest yourself, Lord," I said.

"No, Peter," he said, "my time has come. I must tell you this. I've been wondering. Do you remember that day years ago at Caesarea Philippi? You persuaded me that it was not the will of God for me to go down to Jerusalem and die, and later be raised from the dead?"

I smiled at that silly idea of his about resurrection. "Yes, Lord, I remember."

He gripped my hand even tighter and tried to raise himself off the bed. "Peter, I can't help wondering. What if . . . ?" And then he died.

Ah, it was a magnificent funeral! *Everyone* was there, huge throngs mourning his death.

I must admit that in the years since he died, many of the things we had accomplished for this nation have sort of begun to fall apart. But I guess you can't have everything. At least he was a success during his own lifetime. For thirty years he ruled our people well in Jerusalem, and even a few Gentiles who had heard of him came to consult with him and hear his teachings. He told people many, many stories. (We collected them into a two-volume set; some of you probably have them on your shelves.) But sometimes, like now, when I sit here and look at his silent tomb . . . I too wonder, as he did in his dying moment: what would have happened if he had gone down to Jerusalem and died on a Roman cross at the age of thirty-three?

But I'm awfully glad he didn't.

Aren't you?

The Fastest Gun in the West

This sermon came out of an encounter with the same incident that gave rise to the last one, though this time in Luke's version. It is the crucial encounter of the disciples with the two central realities of their Lord's life, person, and ministry: he was both the Messiah, or the Christ, *and* the suffering servant.

The Christ of God was the one who had long been expected, the one who would come and deliver people from their troubles. The problem is, people tend to blame their troubles on others. In the incident reported in Luke 9:18–25 (and in Matthew 16:13–26 and Mark 8:27–38), Peter identified Jesus as the Christ, the Messiah. But it is immediately obvious, especially in the reports of Matthew and Mark, that he and the rest of the disciples expected Jesus to be the sort of Messiah *they* had in mind, rather than the kind *God* had in mind. Jesus did not come to deliver them from the troubles caused by other people (notably the Romans), but from the troubles they were causing themselves. He did this by dying. That squashed the idea that he was going to be the kind of deliverer they had imagined—or the kind we still imagine, if many of our television shows, movies, or political rhetoric are any indication. His death frees us to see him instead as the kind of deliverer he actually is. More difficult still, it frees us to actually begin to be delivered.

But talking about it in ancient Palestinian terms is boring. We don't really *care* about the history of Jewish expectations of the Messiah, or the realities of the Roman Empire, or the different types of political solutions people proposed for the dilemma of the Jewish nation existing as a client state of that empire. I wanted in my sermon to say something more immediate. Then I realized that the classic myth of the Old West—the town in trouble, and the tall, lean hero who rides in to deliver it—is pretty close to messianic. After I saw that, I went on to develop this story as a sort of allegorical expression of the difference between human messianic hopes and Jesus' vision of God's plan for the Anointed One.

At the end of the sermon I said something like this:

> Years ago Walt Kelly's comic strip character Pogo the possum made a phrase famous. He said, "We have met the enemy, and he is us." It was a potent truism (reminted of course from Commodore Perry's famous dispatch after the battle of Lake Erie, "We have met the enemy, and they are ours"). But there is something more for Christians than that: we have met the Savior, crucified and risen, and in spite of the worst that we have been able to do—to ourselves, to each other, and to him—we have met the Savior, and we are his.

Maybe it wasn't necessary for me to say all that. But I think when you're using allegory, as opposed to a straight story, you need to clue folks in as to what the allegory is *about* . . . I think.

The Fastest Gun in the West
(Luke 9:18–25)

> "The Son of man must suffer many things, and be rejected
> by the elders and chief priests and scribes, and be killed, and
> on the third day be raised" (Luke 9:22).

It's a small town in the Old West—the West of the tall horses
and the mythic heroes. It's high noon; it's hot and it's dusty.
And yet there are a lot of townspeople out—some of them
standing in front of the empty sheriff's office, others lounging
about on the front porch of the dry goods store, some on the
steps of the hotel, and others in the saloon, looking out the
windows from time to time.

One of the children spots it first—a small plume of dust in
the distance, on the trail that leads in from the Great Plains.
Excitement starts to mount in the gathering crowd as the dust
rolls closer and resolves itself into a figure on horseback. "He's
coming! He's coming!" they say to each other, as they move out
into the street and crane for a better view. "The Fastest Gun in
the West is coming at last!"

The townspeople had troubles they didn't know how to
solve, so they sent for the Fastest Gun in the West and asked
him to be their sheriff. With his experience and knowledge, his
courage and his daring, and most of all his legendary speed and

75

skill with his weapons, he will be able to help them. He will deliver them.

Now he's riding down the main street of town, tall and lean, sitting easy on his horse. The noonday sun casts a shadow from the broad-brimmed hat across his face; but folks can see that his eyes are calm and clear, with the serenity of someone who has seen much of life and has come to understand. He rides up to the empty sheriff's office, dismounts, and tethers his horse to the post in front. He looks at the assembled crowd for a moment, then steps onto the porch of the dry goods store and hitches one hip onto the porch railing. For a long moment there's silence. Then he says to them in a voice that could quiet and command a great throng, "You sent for me."

The people look at each other for a moment. What to say? How to explain? Where to begin? The editor of the newspaper steps forward. "We sent for you because we need your help. We don't know what to do. We've got troubles here in town." The Fastest Gun in the West continues to look at him. "I figure it's a gang of outlaws holed up in the hills up there," the editor goes on. "We've been a peaceful town, a town of good people, no wrongdoers, no bad folks; so for years we haven't even needed a sheriff. I figure a bunch of outlaws heard about the town, heard there wasn't any sheriff. I figure it's them that come down at night and do the things that are happening here.

"Well, I'll give you an example. One night I locked up my newspaper office over there and went home. When I returned the next day, the door was still locked; but when I opened it and came inside, the place was a shambles. Somebody had overturned all the boxes of type, paper was scattered across the floor with printer's ink poured on it, and somebody had taken a crowbar to the press. Don't know how long it'll be before I can get the parts to get it fixed. You've got to stop whoever it is that's coming into town and doing these things!"

A tall, gaunt woman pushes her way to the front of the crowd. She's carrying an infant on one arm; a little girl holds onto her hand, and two or three other children cling to her. "It isn't outlaws, Mister," she says to the Fastest Gun in the West. "Something worse! I don't know if you're going to be able to help us. I figure it's things that come out of the graves at night—the undead!—to prey on decent God-fearing folk.

"One night I was sleeping and I heard the most awful screaming, like neither human nor beast—like what people in the old country used to call the 'banshee.' I jumped out of bed, my heart pounding. I lit the lantern and rushed into my children's room and they were all bawling and crying, huddled together on the one bed. They told me some horrible creature had come into the room in the dark and screamed at them. Ordinary bullets won't take care of what's coming after us, Mister. You'll need silver bullets, with crosses on them!"

A boy of about eleven standing near the porch says, "I don't know if it's outlaws, or haunts, or what it is," he says, "but I do know whoever it is has a real bad heart, and you gotta find them. Make them stop doing these things to us, like what they done to me. A lot of people here know that I've been carving in wood for years." Some of the people around the boy nod. "Got pretty good at it," he says. "I've carved cowboys and horses, Indians and tepees. I made a complete town, and all the buildings looked just like the ones you see here. I had just finished the fiftieth of my wood carvings and set it up on the mantel in the living room. I went to bed, and when I got up the next morning, they were all broken. Every one of them! Smashed!" He seems close to tears.

One after the other, the rest of the people begin to speak up. Yes, they've all had similar experiences. Bad things have happened. Folks have started locking their houses at night. They need the help that only the Fastest Gun in the West can give them. After listening for a while, the Fastest Gun in the West stands up, and stillness falls over the crowd. "I'll help you," he says, "but on one condition. I'm not going to be the kind of sheriff that you want; I'm going to be the kind of sheriff that you need. If you'll accept my condition, I'll help you."

The folks look at each other, puzzled. What could he

mean? Slowly they nod their heads in agreement. "All right," he says, "for one week, every night I'm going to walk the streets of your town. One week from today, we'll meet here again and I'll tell you what must be done."

He's about to step down from the porch of the dry goods store to see to his horse when one of the children in the crowd calls out, "Why, he ain't even wearing a gun!" The folks look and sure enough, he isn't. They look over at his horse. There's no rifle scabbard on the saddle.

The editor of the paper pushes his way to the front again. "Just a minute, Mister!" he says. "How do you aim to help us if you ain't even wearing a gun?"

The Fastest Gun in the West—who is unarmed—looks at him. "I wore a gun for years," he says, "and one of the things you find out when you wear one is, it never settles anything permanently. Not anything important, anyway. But gun or not, you agreed: I'm not to be the sheriff you want, but the sheriff you need." Reluctantly, grumbling among themselves, the people disperse. But the next day several people are seen wearing sidearms—if the Fastest Gun in the West isn't wearing a gun, somebody certainly has to.

Night after night the Fastest Gun in the West walks the streets of the town. At first the people feel better just knowing he's out there. But after a few days they realize that bad things are still happening. A man who lives by himself wakes up in the morning with a knot on his forehead as if somebody broke into his house and hit him—but his house is still locked up. Some things get stolen from the dry goods store—without the door being forced. The banker has to tell people that somehow somebody got into the bank and opened the safe and took some of the townspeople's money—but only the banker knows the secret combination.

It's an angry crowd that gathers one week later. Everybody who can carry a gun, including some who shouldn't, is now carrying one. Only the little children and the Fastest Gun in the West remain unarmed.

The Fastest Gun in the West comes out of the sheriff's office, steps onto the porch of the dry goods store, and hitches one hip up on the porch railing. The crowd murmurs. He waits until they get quiet again. "I said I would help you," he says, "and now I will. I have discovered who it is that's doing these things that you hate." There is dead silence in the dusty street. "It is you, yourselves!"

An angry sound comes from the crowd. A number of people reach for their guns. One hand after another comes up and aims a weapon at the Fastest Gun in the West, who carries no weapon. "You, yourselves are the ones who are destroying your own town," he goes on quietly. "You are the ones who are doing evil to yourselves, evil that you blame on others. It is not 'they' who must be stopped; *it is you!*"

Suddenly a barrage of shots rings out. The Fastest Gun in the West makes no move to defend himself; he is slammed back against the wall of the dry goods store and his body slowly crumples to the porch. He is dead.

There's a long silence and then gradually, one by one, the weapons begin to drop in the dust.

The first one to step onto the porch is the boy who carved in wood. "When I saw the bullets hit his body," he says, "I remembered." He turns to his mother and father who stand, ashen faced, at the front of the crowd. "Do you remember how it was when Daddy had all that trouble back East, and we had to move out here and leave our house and all my friends, and Daddy was so sad that we all pretended we were happy to move and happy to change our name? I wasn't happy. Not really! I hated it!

"But I pretended so long that I began to think I didn't. I began to make wood carvings of all the things out here as if I loved them; but I hated them. Only I didn't let myself know it. And when I made the fiftieth one and put it out and went to bed, suddenly all that anger came up and I went out and broke them all, because I hate this place, and I wish we were home!"

The boy stops for a moment, rubs his knuckle in one eye,

and goes on. "But while I was breaking them, I tried to pretend that it was someone else, and after I was finished, I believed that it was—I believed that I didn't do it at all. But when I saw him get hit and smashed by those bullets, I remembered that it was me that hit those carvings and broke them." Then he starts to cry, and his father picks him up off the porch and holds him close.

The gaunt woman steps up and looks down at the shattered body on the porch. "When I heard the sound that the weapons made," she said, "then I remembered, too." She stops, searching the faces before her. "Well, you all know how it is," she says, in a sudden, desperate appeal to the other mothers watching. "Nothing you clean ever stays clean. Nothing you say ever gets listened to. Everything you do has to be done all over again the next day, and from before sunup to long after sundown there's never a moment, never one moment, for yourself!

"You say to yourself, it's okay, it's the best thing in the world to be a wife and a mother. But something inside is crying, hurting, all the time. And one night I got out of bed after hours of lying there awake, and I went into the children's room in the pitch dark and I just screamed and screamed at them. But it wasn't like it was me. It was like it was some awful animal inside me. And when I heard the screaming, I ran back into my own room and lit the lantern and by then I had forgot that it was me that made that awful sound; I forgot it until I heard the sound of the bullets screaming past me just now." A little girl clambers onto the porch, takes her mother's skirt in her hand, puts her thumb in her mouth, and leans up against her legs.

The editor of the paper steps up onto the porch and looks at the blood seeping across the floorboards. "I guess you know by now what I'm going to say. I guess you all have stories that you could tell too," he says, looking at the man with the lump on his forehead, the owner of the dry goods store, the banker.

"My daddy taught me the printing business," the editor

says. "He was from the old country, and he believed in the old ways. When I couldn't find the type in the boxes fast enough, he'd take off his belt and beat me. I thought I had forgotten it, but I guess I hadn't. One evening I came down here—it was like it wasn't even me. I broke everything in sight as if I was hitting back at my daddy for what he did to me when I was a kid. Then I pretended that it really wasn't me—and I believed it."

One by one, the crowd begins to make to each other their own confessions. It takes quite a while.

When they are done, some of them pick up the body of the Fastest Gun in the West—who had learned to walk unarmed—and take him away to rest in peace. The rest follow after him in silence . . . leaving their weapons in the dust.

Who Is the Least?

Who Is the Least?
(Matthew 25:31–46)

"Truly, I say to you, as you did it not to one of the least of these, you did it not to me" (Matt. 25:45).

Once upon a time there was a good man who lived by the law of Christ, the law that demands caring actions toward the poor, the outcast, the forgotten. If someone was sick, this man visited; if someone was hungry, he saw to it that there was food; if someone was naked, he provided for clothing. Wherever there was trouble, he tried to help. He did it as much as possible in secret, so that no one would praise him; as much as possible, he did good so that only God would know of his deeds.

And the good this man did was not only for individuals. Because he was wealthy and because he was influential, he gave his name and his presence and his influence to committees and organizations that attempted to remedy the systemic *causes* of need. Therefore he aided the development of a special crop that would increase the ability of poor soil to produce and resist many common pests and blights; he funded schools and helped create institutes that would develop advanced, creative, and imaginative solutions to problems that were oppressing and destroying people; he encouraged all those he could who sought for ways in which nations might find avenues of peace instead of opportunities for conflict. He was a good man and a righteous man. And one night this good and righteous man had a dream.

This man dreamed that he was in a great wide place, and that in this place there was an enormous throng of people as far as he could see—people from every nation and every tribe under heaven, including people who had lived in the ages past. In fact, so huge was the throng that it seemed to him as if all the people who had ever lived on the face of the earth were standing there, their souls and bodies reunited, all awaiting a word from the great white throne that towered over this place of judgment. Seated on the throne in glory was One who was both human and divine.

Then the judgment began. The peoples of the earth began to be divided, some going to the Judge's right hand and some going to his left. The good man was preparing to step forward, with humble confidence as one who knew that he had lived all of his life by the law of Christ, when suddenly he felt a tug at his sleeve. An old lady, bent over, nearly toothless, was clutching at him with surprising strength and tenacity. As kindly as he could, he said to her, "Please let go of my sleeve; I am about to go to be judged by my Lord."

"You're not ready to go to judgment, young man!" she snapped, and with amazing strength spun him around and pushed him through a little, narrow arch in heaven's wall that was just behind him. He thought for a moment of returning, and yet her words and the fierceness with which she had said them had raised a vague kind of alarm in him. Could it be that she was an oracle or a prophetess? What might she know that he didn't?

He was on a landing. Before him was a circular stone staircase descending into deep gloom within ancient stone walls. He began going down the stairs as carefully as he could, stumbling occasionally on the rough, irregular surfaces. The last dim light fading downward from the plain of judgment failed, and he had to grope from step to step for some minutes in utter darkness. Then he saw the dim glow of a light from around the corner below and ahead of him. The glow grew stronger as he descended, until he came to another landing. There he found a small, heavy wooden door and, in an iron bracket on the wall near it, a flickering torch.

He felt himself drawn forward. He tried the handle—it turned!—and he carefully opened the door. The smell was horrible, as of something left to rot a long time. It was totally dark within. He took the torch from its bracket and, thrusting it ahead of him, stooped through the door into the evil-smelling cell.

The light showed that off in the corner of the cell was a cage, too small for even a little person to stand upright. Crouched within it was something snarling at him, just catching a glint of torchlight in its eyes. He stepped closer, holding the torch in front of him. It was a person! A boy, as well as he could judge. It was unutterably filthy—the hair long and matted, the nails as long as claws, the odor more like death than life. Only guttural sounds issued from it.

The man had read of children abandoned in the wild and raised by animals; the thing in the cage reminded him of such tales. He came closer, intending to release the creature—but then he got a good look at its face.

There was fear on that face. But there was also treachery and deceit and hatred and rage. It was a face that would smile and then moments later grimace with pleasure as the creature crushed a skull with a heavy rock; a face that revealed such animosity as would, if it had the power, destroy every living thing in its path. The good man shrank from such inhuman ferocity and hate, such raw lust for destruction and revenge. Then all at once the thing's feral gaze fastened itself on his own face. He was so unnerved by what he saw in those glinting eyes that the torch slipped from his fingers and caught on a pile of straw. Suddenly the good man was surrounded by a ring of fire—and woke up in bed.

At breakfast that morning he was asked, "What's the matter?"

"Nothing . . . nothing," he said.

"But you look so pale. . . ."

"Nothing!" he said curtly and emphatically. He regretted it. His family was surprised, for he had always been patient and kind. But later that day he snapped at his secretary. She bore it well until she was able to lock herself in the restroom and have a cry, never having heard such a thing from her employer. He was nervous and jumpy all week long, occasionally absent-minded, missing things that people would say to him. He even missed an important meeting of a subcommittee of an agency for international disarmament.

And a week later, in the small hours of the morning, he dreamed again.

Again he stood on the plain of judgment, surrounded by the vast throngs of all ages, and again people began to be divided. He searched his soul as all the peoples of the earth parted and were divided upon the right hand and upon the left of the great figure on the throne. He searched his heart and could think of *no one* who had ever been in need, whom it was within his power to help, whom he had neglected. He was just beginning to take a tentative step forward when a hand fastened on his sleeve again. It was the same old woman.

"*Why do you hold me?*" he all but shouted at her.

"You are not ready for the judgment!" she said to him again.

"But why?" he protested, unable to loosen her grip on him. "I have done good to all to whom I had the opportunity to do good, and far more than most people do! What have I left undone that it was in my power to do?"

"You have done nothing but evil to the 'least of these'!" she hissed, and again she spun him around and shoved him away, so firmly that he almost fell through the little narrow arch in the wall behind him.

Unnerved by her fierce words, he went down again into

the darkness, stumbling on the narrow, twisting stone stairs, until he came again to the landing. He hesitated, then once more seized the torch, turned the handle, and threw open the door. The evil odor beat against his face. "Does she speak of . . . *him*? Is *he* 'the least'?" he asked himself. "But when did I ever see *him* and neglect him?"

Cautiously and fearfully he advanced, the torch before him. He neared the cage. The abject and hideous figure within crouched back against the far bars and growled. Steeling his nerves in spite of his disgust, the good man thrust his hand through the bars—and was bitten to the bone at the base of his thumb! Yelling at the pain, he dropped the torch so that, even as he snatched back the maimed hand, he was again surrounded by a circle of fire . . . and again he woke, sitting bolt upright in his bed, the sweat pouring down his body.

The man spoke to no one at breakfast. On his way to work that day he decided that the only way he could avoid snapping at his secretary was to avoid talking to her except for the most impersonal essentials of business. He did so; and as a result, this time her tears flowed several times while she was sitting at her desk trying to type. He refused all calls and made none. He occupied himself intensely with paperwork and took his lunch at his desk.

As the week wore on, the man became more and more nervous and distracted. It was almost one week from the second dream when, frightened and feeling certain that he would be visited by the same dream a third time, he thought of the old woman in it.

Instantly he was reminded of an old woman he had met several times, one of the oldest members of the church he and his family attended. She was, he remembered, a great-grand-mother, wiser than anyone he had ever met, a great student of the Scriptures, shrewd, and caring to her depths. Without telling anyone, he went to see her. She received him graciously and offered him tea; he accepted. He told her of his dream and, stammering with embarrassment, asked her if she had any idea what it might mean.

"Who is the one in the cage?" she asked, setting down her cup.

"I don't *know!*" he cried.

"I believe you do," she said with astonishing and unapologetic directness. "Because whoever it is, it is obviously someone that you have treated badly and neglected. For he is naked and sick and hungry and in prison, and you never visited him until your dream forced you to; and you have never relieved his distress and never accepted him." Although delivered in a quiet, gentle tone, the words were so harsh as to make him wince—all the more because he knew them to be, somehow, absolutely true.

"But I don't know who that could possibly be."

"Think!" the woman said urgently. "Perhaps when you were young there was someone . . . someone whom no one liked, some child that you hated and avoided and have forgotten about, now that you are grown."

"No . . . no, I can remember everyone who lived on our block. There was no one; no one I played with, no one . . . no! No one at all!"

And that night the dream came again.

This time the good man needed no help from the old woman who again appeared in the dream and reached her bony hand toward him. Before she could touch him, he staggered backward and stumbled through the narrow arch and down the dismal, spiral stone stairway. Coming to the landing, he pushed the door open, yanked the torch from its standard, and entered. He went right up to the bars of the tiny cage and hunkered down there, holding the torch above him and to one side so he could see clearly the hideous face of the one who was, for him, the least of all God's creatures.

Finally he saw it, as the face twisted from the light, snarling. There on the chin—a scar that had resulted from a fall from his tricycle when he was a little boy. The thing in the cage

90

. . . was himself. All his anger and rage and hate and evil; all his treachery; all the bad in him, which he had suppressed and locked away and tried to starve to death and never visited; which he had refused to bring before God for forgiveness but, in his eagerness to be good, had denied and forgotten. All of it had nevertheless survived, and it confronted him now, a forgotten figure imprisoned deep within his own self, his own shadow side.

The man knew, without being told, what he must do. He opened the door of the cage and was viciously, violently attacked by all that he had denied and forgotten. He offered no resistance to the terrible assault. The torch dropped again from his hand, and again he was surrounded by the eternal fire prepared for the devil and his angels. The smoke blinded and choked him. The creature flailed and kicked, clawed and bit and drew blood. Still the man held it close against his heart.

And through the ring of fire (which shrank and died away from that Presence) came the Human One—not sitting on the judgment throne in glory now, but bloody and wounded, despised and forsaken by all, abandoned and forgotten, counted as stricken by God, smitten and afflicted. Through the ring of hellfire, which died before Him as if ashamed, stepped the crucified Jesus, who had borne the grief and rejection and contempt of all humankind.

Jesus surrounded the man and his fearful burden, not with a circle of fire but with his own scarred arms. And the man awoke, beloved by Christ and ready at last to live by Love—the Love he had only known before as Law.

It seems appropriate to place these words of commentary at the end of "Who Is the Least?" instead of at the beginning.

I knew stories could have a powerful impact on people. But the effect of this sermon on one young man in the congregation astounded me. He was a fine man and was active in church ministries. As I was removing my robe after the service, he came down the hallway toward the office. Tears were pouring down his face. He sat down and began to talk.

I admit that I saw no clear connection between what he said to me through his tears and what I thought was the theme of this sermon. But it had made a connection for him. Moreover, he didn't need counsel to sort out his problem, which involved a career decision; he was already doing that well. In fact, I believe that stories actually encourage people to work things out for themselves in a way that standard sermons do not. This sermon seemed to introduce this man to some deep place in himself that he was now for the first time relating to the decision he was facing; that inner meeting proved to be profoundly moving and informative for him.

This sermon resulted partly from reading a paragraph by Ann Belford Ulanov in which she describes C. G. Jung's ability to expose new depths in familiar stories. She speaks of his discussion of the text I subsequently took for this sermon, Christ's parable of the sheep and the goats.

> Christ tells those who marvel at finding themselves among the elect that inasmuch as they show compassion to "the least of the brethren," they show it to him. The essential question to ask, however, is who is the least of the brethren: "What if I should discover that the least amongst them all, the poorest of all the beggars, the most impudent of all the offenders, . . . are within me and . . . that I myself am the enemy who must be loved— what then?" Instead of giving kindness, Jung notes, to this inner

enemy (the "shadow" in his special vocabulary), we scorn it: "Had it been God himself who drew near to us in this despicable form, we should have denied him a thousand times before a single cock had crowed."[1]

---

[1]Ann Belford Ulanov, *The Feminine in Jungian Psychology and in Christian Theology* (Evanston, Ill.: Northwestern University Press, 1971), 129. The passages Ulanov quotes are from Jung's *Modern Man in Search of a Soul,* translated by W. S. Dell and C. F. Baynes (New York: Harcourt, Brace, 1933), 235.

Michal

The first time I read the story of the final encounter between King David and his wife Michal, I was moved by it; I didn't even know why. But I've learned that the stories in Scripture that move me in strange and inexplicable ways should be preached on someday.

When I determined some years later to do a four-sermon series on David, I knew at once that this story would be the text for one of the sermons. I couldn't foresee what would come of it, but another thing I've learned about stories is, it isn't safe to play it too safe: stories that touch me deeply make better sermons if I develop them by following, not leading.

I decided that I would enter into the story and feel my way toward what it meant to me. When I asked myself what my point of view as the narrator should be, I realized I wanted to speak and experience this story from the perspective of Michal. Instantly I knew what she looked like and how she thought—not the historical Michal, of course, but the Michal-of-my-mind. In her book *The Feminine in Jungian Psychology and in Christian Theology*, Ann Belford Ulanov shows that there is a feminine side to the psyche of every man—just as there is a masculine side to the psyche of every woman. In allowing Michal to speak through me, I experienced an aspect of that side of me. As soon as I began to speak, I knew that it was not my regular self speaking, but the Michal-of-my-mind. She spoke fluidly and in a way that convinced me, as I listened to her, that from somewhere inside me I can sometimes intimately understand the experiences and feelings of people, even of the gender that I have never been. I thought for a moment that it might be scary; it was, in fact, exhilarating.

Because the sermon was to be a story, and because I couldn't read to the people all the Scripture necessary to understand it, and because "Michal" looks like a man's name, I gave the following introduction before the reading of the Scripture passage:

> The sermon this morning will be told to you by Michal. That's a woman's name, in Hebrew M-i-c-h-a-l (pronounced MEE-k'l). She was the daughter of Saul and a wife of King David. The story in Scripture is about David's bringing the ark of the covenant up to Jerusalem.

> This was the ark in which the tablets of the law had been put, which had been carried through the wilderness ahead of the people of Israel, which had led the armies of God to victory, which when enclosed in the sacred tent had been the place where God's presence had descended and rested when God wanted to meet with the people. The ark had been taken captive during a battle with the Philistines, but it had caused the Philistines so much trouble that they sent it back. It was kept for a while at the house of a man named Obed-edom, until David finally received word from God that he was to be allowed to bring it up to Jerusalem.

> David did not install it in a temple—that would be the work of his son, Solomon, after him—but he put it again in a tent, the tabernacle. Yet, instead of being in a distant place it was now near the king's house and in the capital of the land.

Michal

(2 Samuel 6:12–23)

As the ark of the LORD came into the city of David, Michal the daughter of Saul looked out of the window, and saw King David leaping and dancing before the LORD; and she despised him in her heart (2 Sam. 6:16).

I am Michal, the daughter of Saul, the wife of David. I have lost the love of David because of my jealousy of David's God. But I should start at the beginning.

Saul, my father, was king in Israel. I was his daughter, one of two sisters and three brothers. And truthfully, I was more like one of the boys than I was like my older sister Merab or the other girls I knew. As I grew older and the other girls were thinking of love and boys, of clothes and babies, I was thinking of war and battles, of government and diplomacy, of rule and kingship. When they were talking with each other about dresses and about the young men they knew, I was talking with my father and my brothers about affairs of state and the ways of the kingdom and the needs of the people.

I had never fallen in love. It seemed to me a silly waste of time. (It was not that I was unattractive. Though I am strong and slender and free, some have told me that I am pretty; but I had no time for such things.) My interest was in policy and statecraft—frustrating things for a woman to be interested in, especially in those times, but they absorbed my attention.

Then I heard of David. Suddenly his name was on everybody's lips: this boy, a mere lad, a stripling, who had been a shepherd of the sheep and at one stroke slew Goliath the Philistine, the greatest military champion who ever lived. I heard the chants as the people followed the troops back into the city that day. "Saul has killed his thousands," they cried out, "and David has killed his tens of thousands!" I saw my father's evil humor start that same day as he heard the praise that went to David—praise which had formerly been his alone. I knew then that David was a man to be reckoned with, that I should pay attention to him, that it might even be well for me to think about fastening my fortunes to his.

But when I went to the banquet given that evening to celebrate our great victory over the Philistines and their giant, I was totally unprepared. When David came into the hall, I turned my eyes to him and felt my heart lurch in my chest. My stomach seemed to drop away from under me. My fingers tingled, my feet felt numb, the room swam in front of my eyes. I scarcely knew what was happening to me, for I had never experienced love for a man before.

What was it about him? He was not tall like my father and my brothers—in fact, David and I stand almost eye to eye. He was not heavily muscled like a career soldier, though he rippled when he walked. He was fair and of a rosy complexion. He was . . . beautiful. I don't think I've even seen a human being as beautiful as he. His mouth was gentle and sensitive; but best of all were his eyes—his deep, dark eyes—which could flash with fire or soften to liquid all in a moment.

I pulled myself together enough to make sure that I sat next to him at the dinner, though once we sat down I could scarcely stammer out a word to him. I, who had always been bold and confident in the company of men! And when he turned and looked at me and spoke to me in that musical voice of his, my heart sang.

By the next day I had recovered my wits, though my heart was lost forever. But I knew enough of policy to know what I must do. I spoke quietly to this one and that one. I sent another one on an errand. I made sure my father got the word. At first he was against it: why would he want David to be a part of his own household—this man whom the people loved more than they loved the king himself? Already that madness was beginning to seize my father that cost him his throne, his kingdom, and finally his life. But one of my servants whispered in his ear: "Marry Michal to David, and she can tell you everything that he plans; that way you can annul his influence among the people." It worked, though I was amazed that my father could be so foolish as to imagine that once I had seen David my loyalty would ever belong to Saul or to his throne again. And so, at last, David and I were married. (I have no words to speak of the first times we were together. Some of you know or remember for yourselves.)

But the madness grew on Saul, and he began to speak to his cronies of seeking David's life. Of course, my people were alert, and word of this was brought to me. Finally one night it was necessary for David to flee, for Saul's assassins had surrounded the house. I knotted the sheets together and helped him out of the window; I put a statue in the bed to confuse and delay those who had come to kill him. By the time they discovered their error, David was far away.

David became an outlaw, and many of the disaffected in the kingdom followed him. My father was enraged with me; he pronounced my marriage to David ended and gave me in marriage to another man. What could I do? A woman had no power then. I went where I was told and did what I must do. But how my heart leaped when I heard stories of the exploits of David, his heroism in the wilderness, his might in battle, his slaughter among our enemies the Philistines!

Years later my father finally died in battle, and David was king, and he sent for me. I left the man with whom I had been living as my husband without a backward glance, though I

99

heard him weeping behind me on the road; and I went again to David.

Some have thought I became jealous because now David had other wives, as was permitted to rich and powerful men in those days. Sharing him with them was difficult for me to learn at first, but I was not jealous of those women! I was smarter and brighter and of more help to David in governing the kingdom than any of them could ever be—and more loyal to him than half of his advisers. No, the jealousy that ate at my heart came from another place. It was a jealousy that had begun in me when I first knew David. I had tried not to think about it and told myself that somehow or another, I would win his heart away from his first love . . . away from God.

But after David became king, he was more infatuated with God than ever. I tried to ignore my jealousy and rage. Here was a man who had never in his life written me a poem, yet I would wake at night to find him sitting by the light of a lamp, his face shining as he wrote love poetry to God! I would see the eagerness in his face when he was going to worship. I would hear him weeping in the nighttime when he thought God had deserted him or was angry with him. To have a flesh-and-blood rival is at least to be able to plot some way of gaining your man back. To have God as your rival is to have no recourse at all! I told myself that he was a fool, that only a lunatic loves God, whom no one can see, who is mightier and greater than all of us. Perhaps that was my jealousy talking.

The matter came to a head the day David brought the ark of the covenant to Jerusalem. He never even spoke to me as he went out to get it, so great was his eagerness. I heard the sound of the procession when it was yet miles off. At last they came into the great square before the king's house, where the tent of meeting had been pitched—the place where the ark was to be put. As they came into the square to the sound of horn and cymbal, to the sound of singing, to the sound of the pipe and the lyre, I saw David. I saw David—who had never danced with me—clad only in a linen loincloth and dancing with all his might before the ark of God. His eyes flashed, his face shone, his body gleamed in the sun as he jumped and spun and turned and whirled in ecstasy . . . before God! I saw a red haze before my eyes. I was furious. I could scarcely breathe.

After the ark was in its place, David came into the king's house to bless the members of his household. I went out and met him outside the door. I shrieked at him so that all the people heard. I didn't care; I was beside myself. I don't know the half of what I said. (I accused him of exposing himself, but I must admit that he did not. The garment he wore was brief, but it was sufficient.) I was wild, I was incensed, I was desperate with past and present loss, with grief and rage and pain. And when I had finished and stood there gasping, he answered me quietly: "It was before the Lord that I danced; and before the Lord I will always make merry."

My rage and jealousy against God have cost me dearly, for I have not seen David from that day to this, though I still live in my rooms in the palace. I saw the look in his eye when I had finished speaking. He looked at me as if I were someone he had never seen before, someone with whom he had nothing in common at all. And it was true. For the greatest passion in David's life was God; but the greatest passion in my life was David. And now I have lost David's love.

I have wept. I have cried out. I have even—to my shame and confusion I confess it—I have even prayed to that same God who stole my life's one love. Last night again, I lay awake all the night long in my grief. Before the sun came up, I was standing and looking out the window toward the eastern hills. The sky gradually began to show the most beautiful rosy hue. It struck me with sadness: it was the same color as the roses in David's cheeks.

And then suddenly my eyes were opened. The God who paints the colors on the sky at the dawning was the one who had painted with beauty the face of the man I loved! The God whose sun rose in splendor was the same God whose light shone in my beloved's eyes. Everything I loved about David had been given him by God; and everything that God had given him had been enhanced by David's love for God. All that I loved in David came from God's gift to him or from his love for God. If he had stopped loving God and turned that love to me instead, as I had wished, what I loved about him *would have been gone!* It was love for God that made David who he was; and yet if I could I would have taken that love away.

Yes, by my jealousy of his love for God, I have lost David's love for me. But somehow I feel that all is not lost; might not the God who loves David love poor, jealous Michal too?

David's heart has closed to me. But perhaps I may yet reach out for the love of David's God.

The Godless Agreement

This sermon was given in Lent, during a series on the Old Testament passages in the lectionary for that year (it was the third Sunday in Lent of year B). Part of that series dealt with God's covenants with us. I called them "agreements" because I can't remember having too clear an idea of what a covenant was before I went to theological seminary, and I assumed that most sermon listeners would find themselves in the same dilemma.

The first part of the series was enjoyable. There were God's agreements with Noah ("the Rainbow Agreement") and with Abraham ("the Sacrifice Agreement")—vivid, memorable, rich in texture and event. But what can you do with the commandments? Here we have the central articulation of the ways in which God wants to relate to us and see us relate to each other; yet most of us cannot manage to feel quite as enthusiastic about God's commands as the psalmist does (Ps. 119:127, 131):

> . . . I love thy commandments
> above gold, above fine gold. . . .
> With open mouth I pant,
> because I long for thy commandments.

Most of us think of the commandments as good for us in the sense that a trip to the dentist or paying our insurance bill is good for us. Few of us have lived long and deeply enough to attain the wisdom that leads to downright love for God's law. At least, that's true for me.

Also, none of us makes "graven images." I mean, not many

103

people are sitting out in the garage nights whittling away at a likeness of Marduk. How can *that* command be applied to *us?* When I was younger I always suspected preachers who told us that our bank accounts or our nation or our job are really idols just like the ones in the Old Testament. I never could *feel* the connection, however much they tried to explain it. Those idols were big old statues you could see and touch and have a rollicking time worshiping; our "idols" were just our way of doing business and were merely things we enjoyed. The connections were awfully abstract; I suspected the preachers of nit-picking. Now that I've grown up and become a preacher, could I make the connections more concrete, more real to my hearers?

Then I recalled that while Moses was up on Mount Sinai getting *these* commandments, his brother Aaron managed to make an idol out of whatever was lying around handy. Might not Aaron still be in business somewhere, doing the same old thing? I began to see a little shop in my mind's eye, and gradually the sign over the door began to emerge. From somewhere in my psyche, a kind of parody of a public relations man began to take shape, wearing an expensive but tasteless sport jacket and smoking a cigar. And standing silently in front of him, half-hidden by mist or cloud, the mountain wind tearing at his cloak and beard, a fierce and powerful old man, whose face seemed to glow through the dimness.

After that, at least for me, the whole business of the commandments stopped being a boring, bothersome obligation that we moderns probably didn't need to hear about anyhow.

The Godless Agreement
(Exodus 20:1–17)

"You shall not make yourself a graven image, or any likeness
of anything that is in heaven above, or that is in the earth
beneath, or that is in the water under the earth; you shall not
bow down to them or serve them; for I the LORD your God am
a jealous God" (Exod. 20:4–5).

Moses, I wonder whether you've realized the terrible public
relations problems it's going to cause if you insist on this clause
about no graven image? If you push this thing, your people
and, later on, the Christians will have *no god* for people to
worship. Oh, of course clever folks like you and me know that
there *is* a God, kind of an invisible Being floating around out
there somewhere. But that doesn't impress a lot of the people
who are our potential clients. They want a god they can see or
touch or visit. They're like children, really; and you know how
hard it is to explain to a child that "there really is a God, honey,
it's just, you know, we can't ever *see* God, really, . . . um,
because. . . . " Well, you know how feeble *that* gets.

Moses, have you given any thought to this? How we'll be
the laughingstock of all the nations if they should ever find out
that we don't *really* have a god there in our temple? I can't
believe you're serious. I mean, *all* the nations have gods! Some
worship a fish, some a goat; one nation worships a rock that fell

from heaven, and one the statue of a pregnant woman. Some nations have *lots* of gods. How's it going to look if we don't even have *one?*

Seriously, Moses, I wish you were more in touch with the needs of the people. Your brother, Aaron, now he did some serious market research, and while you were up there on the mountain dreaming up all these invisible metaphysical marvels, he got busy and built us a golden calf. That's a god people can really get into! I couldn't understand your attitude about it when you came down and saw it; all we're trying to do is just give this new religion of yours some substance, something that we can package and sell to the tourists. You do want this thing to spread a little, don't you?

I mean, Moses, picture the scene down the road a bit. Someday we'll have a country of our own and a capital city and a temple. Now just stay with me on this thing. Imagine some tourist comes to our country from, oh, Babylon or Nineveh or Chicago or someplace. Partly he's just going to want to see the sights. But partly, you know, he's going to be saying to himself, "I wonder if there's anything in this Hebrew religion at all, anything I can take back and share with the folks back home."

Of course he'll tour all the high spots, and that includes a look at the temple. But when he tries to get inside to see our "god," the guide will tell him that nobody is allowed in there. So he'll give up and go along on the rest of the tour, gawking out the windows of the air-conditioned bus. Later on, he'll go out and sample some of the night life. But around two or three in the morning, when everything closes down, he'll be wandering through the streets of the city. He'll see the temple up there, towering above the other buildings and shining in the moonlight. Now, Moses, just about that time he'll probably get a little curious. "Why won't they let anybody in their temple to look at their god?" he'll probably be asking himself. "That must be some special kind of god. I wonder if there's any way I can get in there and have a look for myself."

So he's going to go up there to have a look. And let's say

he finds that at this time of night the temple guards are all asleep. (You still with me on this, Moses?) He crosses the great outer courtyard and enters the inner one. He's impressed by the big altar of sacrifice on its raised steps. He crosses the inner court, goes past the altar, and trots up the steps of the main part. He pushes open one of the tall, heavy doors, just enough to enter. He takes a light from the seven-branched candlestand and crosses to the steps to the Holy of Holies, where he knows we have to be keeping our god. Up he goes, cautiously pushing aside the heavy, embroidered curtains, and slips inside, letting the curtain fall back behind him. Now seriously, Moses, what's he going to think? There'll be no god! No graven image! Oh, there'll be a big box on the floor with a couple of poles stuck through the rings on the side. *But there'll be no statue on it!* He'll think we're crazy.

See, what it is, Moses, this invisible god is all right for you and others like you who are really into theology and stuff like that, but ordinary people like me need something they can get hold of. They need a god they can see, count on, show off to their friends.

So you see, Moses, our imaginary pagan isn't going to understand this temple that doesn't have a god in it. And what's going to happen? Next day, when he's wandering through the bazaar in the old city, listening to the sounds and enjoying the sights, he's going to see the sign on the front of that prosperous little shop:

AARON AND SONS
Your Friendly Neighborhood God Makers

And he's going to step inside.

*
**

"Yes sir, yes sir, what can we do for you?"
"Oh, you startled me! Aaron, is it? . . . Ah! Well, Aaron, I've got a problem. I've been up to the temple, and I've seen how your

brother Moses' religion turns out: there's no god in there for a person to worship. Nothing to really get hold of. Thing is, Aaron, my people back home, they really need a few good gods to worship. I hoped that over here I'd find a god or two I could take back with me, something that would help to make my people more religious, more attracted to going to church, keep the kids moral, and all. But this intangible god your brother is into, well, it just isn't going to sell among the folks back home."

"I quite agree, sir. Frankly, I tried to make that point with Moses, but my brother can be quite stubborn sometimes, and there was just no reasoning with him on this issue. But serving the religious needs of people like you and your friends was just why I set myself up in business. I can provide just the sort of gods you're looking for. Just give me your specifications, and we can make some gods up for you in no time. What sort of gods would you and your people like to have?"

"Well, first of all, a god should be permanent and stable. You can't rely on an invisible god. Make me up a god about, oh, two stories tall, with four bedrooms and two-and-a-half baths, and a nice family room with fireplace."

"Of course, sir. I think we can make something that will be just what you have in mind. And—pardon my asking, but we must make sure our customers are truly religious—how did you plan to worship this god?"

"Oh, that's no problem. I'll dream about it when I'm young, of course. I'll pledge a large portion of my income to it. I'll call it my 'home.' I'll be devoted to it, spending a lot of time every week working on it and making it look nice. What god could ask for more?"

"Oh, *very* good, sir! I can see that you are just the sort of customer Aaron and Sons is looking for. Now then, you said that you and your friends might like some other gods. This 'home' god is only good for one individual or one family. But humans are social creatures, if you don't mind my saying so, sir. Perhaps you'd also like a god that you could share with other people as well?"

"Good idea, Aaron. Make me one out of glass, about a foot tall,

108

with a narrow neck for a cork or cap; fill it with an amber fluid. This one will be easy to worship. In fact, I'll build a worship center for it, with an altar with high seats in front of it for me and the other worshipers, and a mirror behind it with indirect lighting so we can watch ourselves enjoying our god. And I'll be sure to visit this god at least once a day."

"Sir, you are obviously a truly religious person. I suppose you've thought of a god that you can have with you at all times?"

"Yes, in fact I have, Aaron. Make me a god that's portable, about two by three inches so that I can slip it in my wallet. And as it's going to travel with me, it should be made of a durable material . . . say, plastic. Oh, and put my name on it in embossed letters."

"I believe we can make just what you want, sir. And how will you be worshiping this god?"

"Why, whenever I feel needy, I'll take it out and show it to people so I can get just what I want. And people will know what it is, because if I ever look in my wallet and see that it's gone, I'll cry out, 'Oh, my god!' "

"Excellent, sir! And may I suggest, sir, since you seem to be a person on the go, that a number of our clients have expressed satisfaction with our custom-designed gods with four wheels and electronic fuel injection?"

"Sounds great, Aaron! Make me up one or two of those as well. But all these gods are just things, of course. I'm going to want a god that's a bit more personal. Make her beautiful and loving and understanding, Aaron. Before I get her, I will sing hymns to her and 'worship her from afar.' I will expect her to bring me all the happiness I ever wanted, and I will promise to be eternally devoted to her."

"Spoken like a true worshiper, sir. This is an item we don't make here in the shop, of course, and the ordering is a bit uncertain. But we should be able to help you sooner or later, though some of our customers have to try several different models before they're satisfied. And of course, some of your friends will want such a god to be of the masculine persuasion, I believe?"

109

"Of course, Aaron. Right you are. Now, that should be enough gods for a lifetime, I should think."

"Well, perhaps not quite, sir, if I may suggest. Many of our customers return toward the end of their lives and say they wish they had purchased this particular god much earlier." Here Aaron reaches under the counter and brings out a leather-covered, spiral-bound book with a lot of blank pages.

"Hmm! What's this god for?"

"Well, sir, of course you don't begin by worshiping it; that's what you have all these other gods for. But you take pictures of all your gods as you go along and put them in this book. Then, near the end of your life, when your other gods fail you—"

"Fail me? Don't any of these gods of yours come with a lifetime guarantee, Aaron?"

"I'm afraid not sir! That is one problem we have in the god-making business. Sooner or later, no matter how careful we try to be, all our gods give out. That's why we came up with this one, sir. We can't guarantee it, either, of course, but as I was saying, toward the end of your life, you can turn the pages of this god and, ignoring everyone and everything around you, murmur prayers to the images of gods that are gone."

*
**

Well, Moses, there you are. We need some gods that are just a bit more tangible than the One you've come up with. Our marketing people are quite certain of that. So what do you say about all this, Moses? Good ideas, eh?

You shall not make to yourself any graven image of anything. . . . You shall not bow down to them nor worship them.

But why, Moses? Why are you such a stick-in-the-mud about this?

Because you are a person. If you worship a thing, you will become less than a person. If you worship a person, you turn that person into a thing. If you worship your past, you will lose your present and your future.

You shall not bow down to them nor worship them. You are made in the image of God. If you make gods in your own image or in the image of your own desires—if you worship and serve them and take what they have to give—you will lose the only true image of God you can ever have: yourself.

Cain's Story

A number of points in my interpretation of Cain's story were first stimulated by Muriel Pike's poignant and witty one-act drama "Cain" (which I directed once, years ago).[1] One thing that I enjoy about her play is that, as she presents them, that original first family comes across as real people, not just bloodless plaster figures from some never-never land of long ago. She has given new insight to my understanding of that wonderful section of Scripture. Another thing that strikes me in her interpretation is that it never occurs to Cain (as, I suppose, it does not to small children) that hate and rage and jealousy may have consequences. So there is a stunning, unforgettable moment when the characters in the play look— blankly and innocently at first—on the first human corpse the world has ever seen. It is a moment that reaches deep.

First-person sermons are so tempting and rewarding that I keep watching myself so that a majority of my story sermons don't turn out to be told by the central character in some biblical narrative. A fascinating aspect of the method is the opportunity it gives the preacher and the congregation to step inside the skin of a character they had previously seen only from the outside. Even when we don't use first person, it is certainly a handy and revealing device for exploring many passages in the Bible more deeply. The parables, for example, look different from *inside* their various characters than they do from the outside looking in.

---

[1] To my knowledge, the play has never been published; and a recent letter of inquiry to Muriel Pike at her address in England was returned unopened.

I am making an assumption about just what mark God put on Cain. The scriptural narrative says nothing about its nature or location. For the purpose of this story I chose an interpretation that is suggested by an old Jewish legend.[2] When I preached the sermon, I thought it was important to tell the people that ahead of time.

---

[2] See Louis Ginzberg, *Legends of the Bible* (Philadelphia: Jewish Publication Society of America, 5735/1975), 58.

Cain's Story
(Genesis 4:1–16)

And the LORD put a mark on Cain, lest any who came upon
him should kill him (Gen. 4:15).

Don't be alarmed—the mark you see on my forehead is not
what you think it is. It is not evil, but good. It was this mark,
this terrible mark, that finally transformed my life and changed
my heart. But I can see that you are wondering who I am.

I am Cain, your brother. Yes, your brother; for you, like
me, have also felt in your heart the sudden rush of jealousy and
hatred and rage. In my case that fury opened into murder and
poured out the first trickle of the endless river of blood which
the earth has drunk down through the centuries. Perhaps you
have not killed; but has not your heart at times shuddered with
longing for another's death? Yes, we are all brothers and sisters
in the blood.

Long ago, my brother Abel and I lived with our parents,
Adam and Eve, in a land so far away that we thought we were
the only people on the face of the earth. And when we grew big
enough, I became a tiller of the ground like my father Adam
before me, and Abel tended the flocks of sheep and led them in
and out to pasture.

Not long after we had begun working on our own we were

visiting our parents when our father Adam said to us, "My sons, you should offer the first of the fruit of your fields and of your flocks to the Lord." I was surprised that our father would say this, for I had heard his stories about God often. So I said, "Father, this is the same God who drove you and our mother out of Paradise. Why, then, would you want us to worship a God who did that to you?"

Dad thought before answering, then said, "My son Cain, the God who drove me out went with me and has been with me ever since, in my toil, in my labor, and in my suffering. It is this God who has given us all that we have, and it is right to offer some part of it back to God."

Then my brother Abel burst out, "It is not your God, father, who has given me all that I have. It is I, who have worked hard for it! It is my own strength and my own wits that have given me what I have. I owe nothing to God!"

Are you surprised to hear that Abel spoke this way? People think that because I raised my hand against him and slew him, I must be a completely bad person and he must have been a completely good one. But the fact that I murdered him does not mean that he was agreeable or pleasant to be around; in fact, it might argue the opposite!

My father spoke long with us and in the end won us both over. So that spring, for the first time, we prepared to offer back to the Lord something from what we had gained. Abel and I met at a place where my fields and his pasture land joined. There was a hill there. We climbed it together that spring morning, and we worked side by side, each of us building his own altar of the stones that we found upon the hillside. Then each of us made his offering.

The spring of the year in our mild climate was the time of the first barley harvest, so I offered a sheaf of barley, waving it before the Lord as I walked around the altar and then laying it on the fire I had kindled. Abel had brought a firstling from his flock, a young lamb, which he slaughtered, offering the fat

116

parts upon the fire. The smoke of our offerings rose up toward heaven.

And God had regard to Abel's offering, but not to mine.

I did not know that then. It was a while before I found it out. You know, people have said to me in my travels, when I have told them this story, "You must have done something wrong, or God would have blessed you." How little they understand! The universe is not so predictable and easy to fathom as all that; should its Creator be so easy to put in a box? They have said such foolish things to me! "You must have built your altar of undressed stone," one insisted knowingly, "instead of carefully chipping the stones until they fit together just so." But another said to me, "You built your altar, did you not, of dressed stone? Whereas altars to the high God should be built of stones upon which no tool has ever struck." But Abel and I built our altars just the same. Others have said to me, "Abel brought to God of the best of his flock and you probably brought of the most inferior of the grain of your field." But it is not so. True enough, he brought the best lamb from his flock; but I brought the best grain from my field.

And others have said things more foolish still. "Perhaps," one person suggested, "God prefers the smell of burning animal fat over the smell of crisping barley." Can you imagine? "Perhaps," as another with a bit more sophistication put it, "God prefers shepherds to farmers." But what sort of God is that? When we humans are at our best, we make no distinctions among people, but we treat them all fairly; and shall not God, who is the Creator of all, regard us all fairly? Does God prefer one occupation over another? Or city dwellers over those who live in the country? Or males over females? Or one color of skin before another? No. There is no explanation, none that I have ever been able to understand; and I have brooded upon it most of my life since then. No, the most that can be said about it is what I have already said: God had regard to Abel's offering, but not to mine. That's just how things happen.

The way I found out was that there was a drought that

year, and I lost two-thirds of my crop; what remained was scarcely fit to feed to animals, let alone to grind into flour. And when we came again the next spring to that hillside, I was ashamed at the poor offering I had to make to God. As for Abel . . . well, you know how sheep are. They'll eat everything, right down to the ground; it has to be a pretty severe drought before sheep will suffer. So Abel had another fine, fat lamb to offer to God, and his foolish face was smiling and his brow was clear as he greeted me with a show of love. And I began to become angry.

Have you never known this anger? Are you not sisters and brothers to Cain? Oh, it is fine when all is well—when you have your health and your teeth are sound and your work is succeeding and your children are respectful and your spouse is kind and loving to you. Then *you* can be loving toward the whole universe. But when things begin to go wrong and you look from your pit of misery at the smug and smiling and successful faces of others, have you not known rage and jealousy? I was angry with God for blessing Abel and not me. But God was not there. So my anger found a closer focus.

"Come," I said to Abel, while the fire was consuming our offerings. "Come aside with me into the field" . . . my field. For I remembered something I had seen there. And there it was, lying on the ground as we came to the foot of the hill. I picked it up. It was a rock, shaped just so. A while later, when I looked at it again, the end of it was wet and red, and my brother lay upon the ground. And yet it was not my brother, for he neither moved nor spoke, and the earth—the dry and drought-stricken earth—had opened its mouth to drink his blood. I dropped the rock on the ground beside him and went back up to the top of the hill.

The fires were out, and the altars gave off smoke that mingled with dark, low-hanging clouds. Thunder came from the clouds. I seemed to hear amid the thunder a word: "Brother." But I did not know where my brother was! That was not my brother, that which lay in the field at the foot of the hill.

118

My brother was gone. I had reached out and taken my brother's life in my hand, but I had not been able to keep it. I could not keep my brother, and I did not know where he was.

I fled from those altars. I buried what remained of Abel. I tried to go on farming, but every time I thrust the blade of the plow into the ground, it was as if I were thrusting it into my brother's body, and the ground seemed to cry out to me in pain. After a while it got so I could hear that cry in the middle of the night, so I left off farming and fled. I became a wanderer on the face of the earth, hoping that someone would kill me as I had killed my brother. I deserved it, and it would end this terrible guilt that I carried with me everywhere.

After several days of wandering, hungry and alone, I came one evening to a campfire. It was a group of shepherds . . . like my brother. I approached them, and they rose up against me— for in those days, a stranger was feared. They had stones in their hands. *How just,* I thought! *Now these shepherds will kill me, just as I killed Abel, and then God will be satisfied.* But when I came fully into the firelight, they looked at me and dropped their stones and backed away, and they pleaded with me to leave them. I didn't understand. I said to them, "I am hungry," and I backed out of the firelight. One of the oldest of them, trembling, brought me some of their stew meat wrapped in leaves and left it at the edge of the circle of the light. I picked it up and went on my way, wondering how it was that my life had been spared. It happened that way several times, and still I didn't understand, until the day I went to drink from a pool formed by a mountain stream. There I saw, for the first time, a reflection of my own face, and this mark which you see—the white patch upon my forehead—the sign of the leper.

I was horrified, and then I became more enraged at God than ever. God, who had rejected my offering; God, who had refused to bless my labors; God, who had punished me with this terrible banishment from friends and kin and from the rich and growing earth, but would not grant me death—this same God now had also stricken me with leprosy! And yet . . . the patch never spread, and it had feeling in it, so it was not what I feared. Nevertheless, others still thought it was, and they feared and avoided me. Thus my spirit still sickened within me, making me bitter toward the God who hounded me, isolating me in this living death.

Then one day I came to a village in my wandering, and the villagers came out to drive the stranger away. But they backed away from me as usual when they saw the mark upon me. And suddenly I found myself calling to them, "It is not what you think! It is the mark of a high and mighty God, and it has been placed upon me to protect and defend my life. God in mercy has protected me."

Do you know, I never thought those words before I said them. But after I said them, I saw how true they were. "God in mercy has protected me." I still do not understand the ways of the universe or of God, and I wish—oh, how I wish!—that God had blessed my labors and my work. I wish that God had had regard to my offering. I wish that God had favored me. And I wish . . . and I wish that I had not killed my brother.

But sisters and brothers of Cain, I have found something better than God's blessing, something better than God's favor. *It is God's mercy, and God's love.* For not all are blessed and favored: some are wise and some are foolish; some are well and some are ill; some are strong and some are weak. But all alike are loved. All alike are loved by the merciful God who has guarded me and watched over me and cared for me all my days, killer that I am.

And that is the true reason why we are all brothers and sisters, you and I. Not because any one of us might kill (though that is true), but because all of us, favored or not, are loved by God.

The Day Jesus Came to the City

This was a Palm Sunday sermon. I found it fascinating to compose and to tell. The congregation seemed quite absorbed. The organist began crying toward the end, which she said embarrassed her—she sits in plain view of the congregation in the church where I first gave this. Even so, she liked it and asked for more like it.

I told the story again to a different congregation. For some reason my faith in the story and in the hearers faltered, and I sank, like Simon Peter, into a sea of explanatory comments. I began by saying, "When Jesus comes into Jerusalem, he encounters different kinds of people. When Jesus enters the city of our life, he encounters different aspects of our personality. The first character he will meet is our worldly shrewdness."

I don't know why I sometimes get so fainthearted when I go to preach a story. I know other preachers do too, but that scarcely excuses chopping a story sermon into bits with intrusive "clarification." It sounds like *Pilgrim's Progress* at its worst, doesn't it?—"Mr. Worldly-Shrewdness" and so on. I bet nobody was much moved by it the second time; and no wonder, with me trotting on stage after every character, with placards that said the equivalent of "This is what that just meant, and now here is what this next bit is going to mean." Ugh! I should leave that for the standard sermon. The point of a story is not to have a "point," but to provide an opportunity for an experience. After experiencing a real story, we can make "points" for ourselves.

The Day Jesus Came to the City

(Matthew 21:1–17)

"Tell the daughter of Zion,
Behold, your king is coming to you,
humble, and mounted on an ass,
and on a colt, the foal of an ass" (Matt. 21:5).

I'm a Roman soldier, part of the army of occupation in Jerusalem, here to keep the peace. Rome's peace. I was on duty that day, keeping watch from the parapet of the southeast tower of the Antonia Fortress. I had a good view over the temple area. The fortress was built right next to the temple so we could keep watch on the Jewish crowds on their festival days. Sometimes they got pretty worked up at those festivals.

From where I stood I could actually look *down* on that little hill they call the "Mount" of Olives. I was watching the mobs of pilgrims coming along the road, singing and chanting, when suddenly I noticed a large group of people coming around the southern corner of the "mount." In the middle of them I could make out a man sitting on a donkey. That seems harmless enough, doesn't it? And yet, I don't know why, some soldier's instinct made me rest my hand on the hilt of my sword. I could hear them chanting something over and over again, but I didn't know their language well enough to make out what it was. As I was trying to figure out what they were yelling, I heard a step behind me.

I turned around, and there was the procurator, Pontius Pilate himself, come to see what it was all about. I gave him my soldier's salute, and he told me to stand at ease. The two of us stood there at my guard post in silence, watching the procession move nearer along the flank of that little hill. All at once he spoke to me. "Soldier, do you understand what they're saying?"

"No sir," I replied. "I'm no student of their language. I just know a few words for haggling in the shops."

"I have studied it," he said thoughtfully. "They're calling out 'Hosanna!' It's an ancient Hebrew word. It means 'Save us!' They used to shout it to their kings. The last time there was a rebellion here in Palestine, the rebels shouted 'Hosanna' to their chief when he led them into battle. Perhaps they thought that by shouting that they could make him king. He ended up on a cross."

The procurator was silent for a moment, watching the shouting, singing crowd starting to cross the little valley that lies just on the other side of the temple walls. Still watching them, he asked me, "What's the first thing they had you say, back when you took your soldier's oath?"

Without having to think, I replied, "There is no king but Caesar."

"That's right, soldier! Caesar—the emperor—is what holds the whole empire together. It's loyalty to Caesar that ultimately keeps the Roman peace across half the world. Oh, sometimes a country gets to keep its little kinglet, provided he always bows toward Rome. But the Jews are not allowed a king; they are prickly and troublesome enough as it is."

Pilate peered down as the procession drew nearer the great gate into the temple courtyard. "I think I know who that is who's being hailed as the king of the Jews this fine spring morning. I've had reports on him. I hope I won't have to have a confrontation with him. But if I do . . . "

124

The procurator let the sentence hang and walked away and down the stairs. I thought, *He's right! There is no king but Caesar: no king but whoever gives you your job and pays you your salary and maintains the roads and controls the army and keeps order and levies taxes and has the power of life and death. And if this fellow on the donkey thinks he is a king, well, he will learn differently at the end of a Roman lash, or maybe even hanging from a Roman cross.*

It was then I remembered that according to the roster, I was on execution duty at week's end. *Well,* I thought, *there'll be work to do before this week is out.*

*
* *

I'm a priest in the temple at Jerusalem. I trained here to be a priest since I was a boy eight or nine years old. I love the temple, and I love the religion of our ancestors. I was hurrying across the temple courtyard on that particular day to see to some duty or make some arrangements; the holy season of the Passover is a busy time for those of us who are ministers in God's house. There were knots of pilgrims everywhere, impeding my progress: changing filthy Roman money for the pure temple coins; buying their animals for sacrifice; and some of them just standing there, rapt, with their hands up as they prayed to God in front of God's own house. Suddenly one of the temple guards, dodging through the people, ran up to me. I must have been the first priest he saw, for he said, "Come quickly! There may be trouble!"

I followed the guard to his duty station on top of the wall that looks east toward Mount Olivet. There I saw the procession coming toward the great gate. There was a man on a donkey, surrounded by a throng of people, many of them shouting the ancient greeting to a king—"Hosanna!"—and waving palm branches and spreading their outer garments on the roadway in front of him.

"Do you know who it is?" asked the guard.

"Yes," I said, recognizing at once that unforgettable face. "I heard him once . . . the last time he was in Jerusalem." I was remembering: one of those awful Samaritans was there that day, defiling the holy city by his very presence. "Master," the depraved apostate whined, "we worship on our mountain north in Samaria, but you Jews say we should worship at this temple here in Jerusalem. Now, which is right?" And I remembered Jesus' answer, and the shock it gave me: "Neither on that mountain nor in this temple," he said, "for God is a spirit, and those who worship God must worship in spirit and in truth."

The temple is my life, the life of so many of us who serve here, the heart of our religion, the center of a nation's worship. It is the temple that holds the nation together. It's all we have now against the power and paganism of the Romans, with their many gods which are no god. And to this man the temple was of no importance! Think of what we have sacrificed to have these walls, to hold our worship here; but he said we must worship God, not in the temple, but "in truth"! Who is worthy enough to worship "in truth"? What does it mean? I was afraid there would be trouble with this man, that he would stir the people to riot and bring Roman troops from the Antonia Fortress crashing into the sacred precincts of God's house during this holy season. The temple authorities could not ignore someone who threatened everything that is most sacred and holy to us.

*
**

I was just a little child at that Passover festival when Jesus came to the city. It's the first Passover I remember going up to Jerusalem. We had walked many miles to get there, and as we came near the great walls, my uncle was carrying me on his shoulders. We heard a lot of people shouting, "Hosanna! Hosanna!" So everyone stepped to the side of the road as a kind of a parade started to come by. There were people waving branches and throwing dust in the air—it made me rub my eyes—and shouting and singing. A man on a donkey came right close to us, and when I saw his eyes, saw the look in his eyes, I just stretched out my arms to him and shouted, "Hosanna!" like everybody else. And he smiled and reached out his arms to me. My uncle lifted me over his head and gave me to him, calling out, "Jesus, take good care of her!" The man nodded to my uncle and smiled again at me. Then he held me close, and I put my head against his chest, where I could feel his heart beating.

So I rode with him into the city. I don't remember what happened after that. I wasn't there to see all the troubles Jesus had later. But afterward our whole family joined his disciples, and so I have been one of his followers ever since. Some people say he's going to come back soon, very soon, and make the world a better place. Some people say he won't come back for a long time, so we must work to make the world a better place for him meanwhile. I don't know which is right. But I do know that when he comes back, I would like to sit close to him again . . . close to his heart.

*
**

I am a donkey. I know you will smile, and some of you will laugh, because donkeys are funny. People always smile and laugh when they see us. When I was just a little colt, there were some children who would come over to my owner's place and play with me. And after they had played with me for a while, they would start to sing songs, and then they would call to me, "Sing, donkey, sing!" I would sing as well as I could, but they would laugh and laugh at my funny voice and throw things at me. It was worst when they threw mud at me, because mud sticks.

One day two men came and they talked to my owner and then they took me away to where there were a lot of people. A man came to me, and they put a soft cloak on me, and he got up and sat on me. I was scared because no one had ever ridden me before. But he leaned forward and put his arms around my neck, and he said something in my ear, something that I've forgotten. But after that I wasn't scared any more. They led me along, with him riding on my back, and even though people were shouting right next to my ear and waving things in front of my face and throwing things on the road in front of me, I wasn't scared, because he kept his hand on me all the time. When the ride was over, they took me back to where my owner lived.

Days later—I remember it because it got real dark that day and the earth shook underneath my hooves and there was thunder—the two men came by again and they talked to my owner, and they said, "He's dead." I thought they were talking about the man who had ridden on my back. But they couldn't have been, because two days later, early in the morning before the sun came up, I was in the orchard eating figs that had dropped from the trees, and I heard something. It was the sound of someone walking barefoot through the dew. He came and stood next to me. At first I didn't know who it was because he didn't smell the way he had smelled before. He smelled like blood and death. But then he put his arms around my neck just the way he did before, and he whispered in my ear. This time I remember what he said: "Thank you for letting me ride you."

I haven't seen him since, but if he ever wants to ride me anywhere ever again, he can.